POWER
YOUR
DECISIONS

SELF-STUDY WORKBOOK

A Personalized Roadmap
to Success

DR. PAMELA D. GREY

POWER YOUR DECISIONS SELF-STUDY WORKBOOK

A Personalized Roadmap to Success

Revised edition 2023; Original copyright © 2019 Pamela D. Grey

Published by Advancing Mind & Spirit, LLC

Dr. Pamela D. Grey

ISBN: 979-8-9887448-0-1
Library of Congress Control Number: 2023914523

Printed in the United States of America

Copyright permission to use references to *The Power of Decision* book and other books by Raymond Charles Barker, author, granted by Rev. Dr. Lloyd George Tupper.

Book Cover Design: Jahnava Alyssa Baltz

Book Design: David Smith M.F.A. and Dr. Pamela D. Grey

Printing History:
October 2023: Second Edition
June 2019: First Edition

Special Recognition: Rev. Lloyd George Tupper, D.D., and Dr. Denise Federer, Ph.D.

The mission of the Advancing Mind Foundation is supported by this publication. Go to www.advancingmind.org for more information.

For more information and additional resources, including our inspirational monthly newsletter, go to:

www.poweryourdecisions.com

Who Wants to Make Better Decisions?

Power Your Decisions is a contemporary study in how to make spiritually grounded decisions. Spiritual thinking can help you tackle everyday problems and achieve your long-term aspirations with greater ease. Desiring to do both is truly a big step in the right direction.

This workbook was inspired by the writings of a remarkable spiritual mentor, teacher, and author, Dr. Raymond Charles Barker, who gave his audiences the **Letter of the Law** in his writings. He wrote about a spiritual life intimately entwined with a creative process that only decisions could ignite. But sadly, his passing in 1988 left audiences without the required knowledge to ignite those decisions and put his wisdom into daily practice. Too many people were left to their own devices to figure it all out by themselves – until now. With this personalized self-study, you now have the **Spirit of the Law** in a well-constructed roadmap to help you confidently cross that intersection. You have the whole foundation of knowledge required to apply his wisdom and make better decisions for a lifetime of greater success.

Striving for success can be a lifelong challenge without the proper guidance to navigate through the barriers that limit your opportunities. That is why a reliable roadmap is so important. When you can see yourself identifying what is important to you, making more positive choices, and thinking with greater clarity, you have made a big leap in improving your whole mindset – the key for succeeding in any endeavor. Knowing you have a pathway to the open road helps you achieve personal progress with more confidence. You now have a compass and map to help you navigate the open road ahead. As you arrive at new and deeper truths about yourself, expect this journey to reveal new and inspiring goals along with new ideas to achieve them. Amazing summits of opportunity await you in the days ahead. I will show you how you can now become part of the next generation of great decision-makers by staying on this path.

Why New Generations Need a Better Roadmap to Succeed!

My whole life changed once I began to study the New Thought giants of the twentieth and twenty-first centuries. I later had the privilege of working alongside some of them as well. Their achievements and contributions are legendary to many. My work here has been especially inspired by the writings of Dr. Raymond Charles Barker and the personal mentoring and spiritual leadership of Rev. Dr. Lloyd George Tupper, himself a Minister and Practitioner of 50+ years, who took classes from Dr. Barker and considered him a mentor. Sadly Dr. Barker and other twentieth-century spiritual leaders like him are not alive today to teach the more difficult concepts, spiritual practices, and even the vocabulary used in their time. There are few experienced or trained teachers in New Thought practices and principles to offer people a solid foundation of knowledge and best practices. *Power Your Decisions* bridges that gap as a self-study, on-the-go workbook.

With a step-by-step workbook format, I have helped many adults and faithful readers find easier ways to achieve personal growth. Many of the exercises in these chapters illustrate the ways I learned to use and understand these concepts and principles. With time and practice, many factored into some of my most important decisions – like writing this workbook. It became evident to me new generations and people of all ages were in need of finding a better way to make their most important decisions. And once they adopted a new framework for thinking and living, they could significantly impact their success and achievements over their lifetimes.

I was also determined to write a workbook for anyone who desired to learn the foundation of spiritual thinking, grounded in real and accurate terminology, in a self-study format. It had to be comprehensive but not daunting to complete. I finally focused on eight lessons to help every person gain mastery of spiritual concepts while also helping them make better decisions.

No longer will unproductive habits and choices place limitations on anyone's results. Everyone can now learn a way out of problematic thinking by letting go of inferior thoughts that cause delays to having better results. Take time to digest new material, think about how it applies to your goals, and read everything with an open mind. You will be introduced to the importance of spiritual reflections, practices, and applications that aid in the whole decision-making process. Your best decisions are truly intertwined with your spiritual growth and understanding. Remind yourself, this is not a quick fix, but a new way to live your life.

This self-study experience will help you choose your thoughts and words more carefully. Be open to improving your relationship with the God of your understanding so you can truly know what God is and is doing in your life; this will be very important. Later workbook chapters will teach you an affirmative prayer, or what is called a Spiritual Mind Treatment, to enhance your spiritual development as well. You will learn to gather better ideas that will help you make better decisions affecting your career, health, finances, creativity, and love life! Once you understand how to use the power behind every decision, your life will never be the same! That is not hyperbole, that is a promise!

All my best,
Dr. Pamela D. Grey
Author, Mentor, and Businesswoman

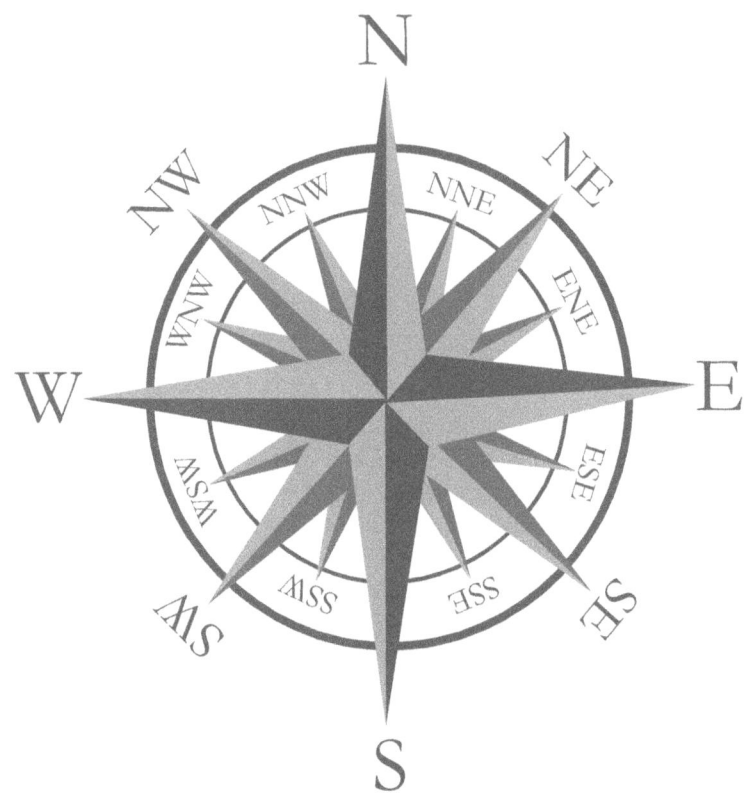

In which direction do you want to go?

Introduction

It is a privilege and joy for me to write the introduction to a workbook I have long waited to see published. At no time in my fifty-year career as a Religious Scientist and Minister have I seen the principles of decision making written in such a simplified and yet comprehensive manner. Anyone who reads this workbook will find their life greatly enhanced and all their decisions empowered.

My dear friend and colleague, Dr. Pamela Grey, has taken the concepts, ideas, and application of decision making to new heights in this self-study workbook, having applied them to achieve a brilliant career in her own right. You now have the same opportunity to experience your own inner genius as was given to her when she found inspiration in the classic *The Power of Decision* by Dr. Raymond Charles Barker.

I first met Dr. Barker in 1968 at The First Church of Religious Science in New York City. I soon became his student and eventually his friend. As a minister I taught and lectured on the principles put forth in his books. *The Power of Decision* never failed to deliver significant impact and influence to its readers. Now five decades later, Dr. Grey has created a world-class study in consciousness with her *Power Your Decisions Workbook*. I am confident in saying that Dr. Barker would be proud of a new voice that can bring his ideas to a wider audience and create a new generation of great decision makers. Dr. Grey brings inspired, new insights to the study of classic wisdom traditions.

I first met Dr. Grey when I was President of The Holmes Institute in Los Angeles, California. Our Board of Trustees hired her to launch a new Master's Program in Consciousness Studies. As the Director of Distance

Learning, Dr. Grey worked tirelessly alongside our world-class faculty to make our new program in Consciousness Studies a success throughout the country. The Institute, founded in 1972, has graduated hundreds of ministers for the Centers for Spiritual Living throughout the world.

Dr. Ernest Holmes, author of *The Science of Mind*, once wrote, "The All Creative Medium [God] does not think one thing is easy and another thing is difficult. With God all things are possible. We must know this and this Power of God must be hooked up with our thought, with what we are doing. Energy unconnected does nothing. It is only when it is used, properly directed, that it accomplishes things."

If you want to succeed, prosper, and be happy, get inwardly connected, be properly directed, and make your inspired decisions. Whatever you do to make your next decision grow into form, I wholeheartedly encourage you to use Dr. Grey's wonderful workbook to guide you through each step of the process.

Rev. Dr. Lloyd George Tupper
Chatham, Massachusetts

Workbook Contents

Considering a Change in Your Life?

o you want a more balanced life? Are you trying to create a better pattern for health? Are you seeking more prosperity or a greater expression of your gifts and talents? When these elements are in balance, life is good. But when one of these areas is out of order, something inside you is being neglected. A balanced life sounds nice, but you have to work to achieve it. How? You have to learn how to let go of lesser conditions that no longer serve you. When you do, you will find you don't have to be perfect in your thinking. You only have to begin to think correctly.

Don't Accept Inferior Thoughts That Lead to Lesser Conditions

Exploring one new idea about yourself can expose a static condition in your life. When an old pattern of thought no longer serves you, releasing it allows you to make a change. This workbook gives you insightful assessments to identify these static conditions that are caused by inferior thinking. If left unchecked, these inferior thoughts can expand to drain your energy and lead to poor health, difficult relationships, and financial stress, which can make you feel unworthy. Each of these revealing patterns will always lead to lesser conditions that won't support your growth. You can push all of these aside and stop dwelling on the negatives. Your answers to these conditions are within reach. Discover that these conditions and problems were never going to improve your life. Instead, learn to solve them by eliminating inferior thoughts and stopping the routine neglect of your personal needs. But what starts you down a pathway of neglect? What are those static conditions? It's been said that if you are experiencing frustration,

1

it means you are forcing your willpower to change a condition in your life. Isn't it time you stop working on problems alone and discover your inner talents? Once you learn that perfect ideas are your birthright, you start thinking correctly to solve your challenging situations. But how do you think correctly?

Your Mind Is Your Greatest Asset!

First, you must stop analyzing the past for solutions. Your problems aren't here to improve you, so trying harder while going in the wrong direction isn't the answer. This workbook is offering life-nourishing principles to navigate you further into discovering your inner genius. It's here you will find all the greatest ideas meant to lead you out of your present circumstances. Thoughts void of answers or inferior thinking will soon be discarded when you begin to practice how to think correctly. Focus on the step-by-step instruction put forth in this self-study, and soon you will master new decision-making skills for a lifetime of remarkable benefits. Learn how to grow a creative consciousness so you can experience a better way to live out your dreams. Stop trying to solve all your problems with only your limited human mind. Discover how your mind is part of a Universal Intelligence which exists for your benefit. Unveil a personalized roadmap for success inside you when you complete the exercises in *Power Your Decisions* and fulfill your greatest ideas in an easy-to-follow instructional format.

Dr. Barker declared in his 1957 book *The Science of Successful Living*, "the aim of all religion and education was to increase the area of human consciousness." He would later write about these two systems in one of his most acclaimed books, *The Power of Decision*, stating that, "Too many religious systems have taught doctrines of repression," which he believed often crippled its adherents psychologically and limited their self-expression. The movement he helped to lead in America raised the "creative consciousness" of individuals and offered a divinely balanced process for everyone to grow spiritually, no matter their circumstances.

A Better Roadmap Will Take You Where You Want to Go

T he task of making better decisions does not take time, it takes practice. A better roadmap should give you enough practice to help you avoid the unwanted detours in life, the ones that distract you from your goals, limit your quality of life, or hold you back from true satisfaction. Even high achievers need help sometimes. They know their tool box of ideas and resources is insufficient to offer direction. "If only I could find a better way," they say to themselves. I am not a clairvoyant, but to achieve better results, most people must overcome one or two personal challenges. That is why this workbook is so helpful; you work through things and learn to eliminate those road blocks. A roadmap is only as good as the results you get, proving you have navigated the journey successfully. However, in this self-study you cannot mimic the road map. *You must embody it.*

When you open yourself up to a whole different journey that affords self-discovery, you soon see life with fresh eyes. *In truth, you become a humble person and the best audience for this self-study, because you are the most teachable.* You know you don't know and very much want to learn. By being teachable, you also absorb new material well. You are fortunate to be a willing person, another good sign you can navigate this roadmap successfully. That means you are willing to tackle some of the greater personal challenges to realize better results. Well, when the student is ready, the teacher appears. So, that makes your need for help and my workbook the perfect pairing to reach your destination!

While this workbook will not solve all your problems, it will help you move beyond many of them. Better ideas and better tools do give you a great advantage. And why not reach for the stars? After all, you a very fortunate person indeed. Fortunate because you are humble, you are willing, and you are teachable, some of the better qualities to succeed in any journey. Now, the only thing you need is a better roadmap.

Here's How to Get Started!

Because all roadmaps have a starting point, begin slowly, and take your time! You can speed up in later chapters. Remember, this journey is about going places you have not explored before. Some information will be unfamiliar to you. You will be asked to write down what you have learned and journal your impressions. This will help you gain clarity and achieve a better understanding of what you did not know about yourself before. This workbook is organized like a puzzle; everything fits sequentially together. Do not throw one piece out or skip over new material, especially in the first half of this workbook. That is where foundational information and essential vocabulary will be presented to you. Before long, most words will take on new meaning and a larger role in how you make better decisions. Each chapter is organized into six practical steps, starting with a review of what you believe. Do not skip around, as there are many good reasons each chapter is organized the way it is. By the end of this self-study, your goal will be to reveal a well-organized picture of yourself, piece by piece. Your exercises and reviews are practice opportunities, and by examining your circumstances in real time, you are likely to discover new puzzle pieces you did not see before or thought were missing. Lastly, throughout your self-study, keep an open mind to allow all the moving parts of your *body, mind, and Spirit* to come together. When they do, you will experience a better you through the benefits of better results. Let's get started!

Follow These Six Steps to Create a Personal Roadmap

Ask Yourself: "What Do I Believe?"

Your answers reveal the values, beliefs, and even something about your behaviors as you undertake this journey.

Read a Unique Chapter Summary

Examine one area of your life through a new lens. See where you can improve your thinking to achieve a better result.

Get Ready to Adopt New Material

You will be presented with a vocabulary of familiar words described and applied in new ways.

Journal Your Impressions

Capture nuggets of wisdom through each new personal discovery. What did you not see before? What opened your eyes?

Personalized Workbook
Exercises and Assessments

Think back about how you have chosen to evolve personally. Your life experiences have brought you to where you are today. Are you preparing for new ideas or struggling with the old ones? Use these exercises to find new and lasting ways you can improve all your future decisions!

Takeaways on Making Better Decisions

Arriving at your next big decision does not take time, it takes practice. Success will always leave a trail of new clues once you apply the power of decision to all areas of your life!

Barkerisms

Here is a sample of how you will see Barkerisms presented throughout the workbook. These are exceptional, potent statements used frequently by Dr. Barker. They were so popular they eventually became known as "Barkerisms" and were popularized in all his lectures and books.

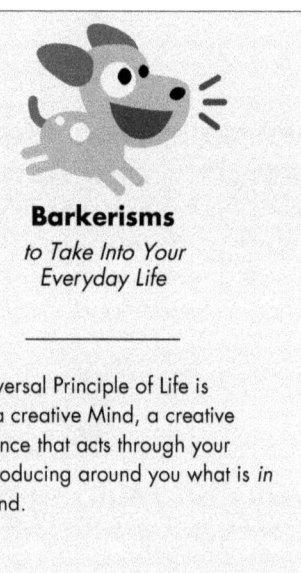

Barkerisms
*to Take Into Your
Everyday Life*

The universal Principle of Life is that of a creative Mind, a creative Intelligence that acts through your mind producing around you what is *in* your mind.

Barky

Take a Spiritual Guide Dog on Your Journey

Barky is an imaginary offspring of Dr. Barker's *Barkerisms* as described in the vocabulary section on page 11. Consider Barky your spiritual guide dog on your journey throughout this workbook. He points to new ways to achieve better results in your life. Barky wants you to be as excited and passionate as he is about your journey! Forget a leash; he doesn't need one. And neither do you to unleash remarkable ideas to fulfill your potential!

Magical Barky *helps you see the world in a bigger way. There is magic in a new idea that can transform your life!*

Happy Barky *will make you laugh and smile. He wants you to enjoy success!*

Baby Barky *shows you baby steps are often needed before you can move forward with confidence!*

Pointer Barky *points you to seriously important phrases and key subject matter. Follow his lead; he won't lead you astray.*

Quizzical Barky *will help you dig deeper into new and rewarding ideas. He finds so many nuggets of wisdom that are out in the open for your taking!*

Thumbs-Up Barky *tells you it's a great idea to start applying your self-study to your daily activities of living.*

Mountaineer Barky *wants to take you to new heights and summits to help realize your greatest gifts and dreams!*

New Phrases
and Words

Dr. Barker explained that in every new area of science, new words, phrases, and whole new terminologies are necessary. Now you have at your fingertips a contemporary vocabulary to help you get acquainted with a mental science – the science of New Thought. Discover for yourself how the power of spiritual thinking not only helps you achieve better decisions but changes the quality of all the results you get for the rest of your life.

Let Go of the Old to Bring in the New!

Older, well-known books written by many great leaders of the New Thought movement are dense in their content and even more difficult to read because of older terminology. Even words we use today were not known at the time, and many were not well explained then or now. With this workbook, you have a well-constructed guide, a roadmap you can easily navigate, along with exercises that will help you practice. Once you begin to understand how an essential new vocabulary fits into the future of your decision-making, you won't leave home with it.

It can be tough letting go of what no longer serves you. Older thoughts like older terminology often have to be released before you can replace them with new ideas and fresh plans. That is why you are here – to let go of problematic thoughts and raise your awareness about new ways to improve yourself in the process. While you came to where you are today by doing the best you can, now you have an opportunity to discover new qualities about yourself, many you have not fully tapped into before. These may even be greater qualities that you ever thought existed. It's time you stop delaying your good and get rid of those outdated patterns holding you back. With this self-study, you will get there much faster and with less trial and error.

Practice Your New Vocabulary Each Day

Start practicing a new vocabulary the minute you begin this self-study. You will also have many opportunities to write out what you understand about these words in the chapters ahead. This is intentional. Making a better decision doesn't take time, it takes practice. By practicing each new word, concept, or phrase, you can speed up the time it will take you to make your next best decision. Trained thought is much more powerful than untrained thought. Now is your opportunity to begin that training – just like other skills and practices you will be exposed to in this study. You will enjoy the journey better when you know what you are doing and why you are doing it.

Affirmative Prayer: God's fresh ideas are what you are seeking when you undertake an affirmative prayer. To affirm to yourself out loud or silently is to make a positive declaration or announcement. When you pray, you believe in a positive concept of a loving God. Dr. Ernest Holmes, a pioneer in the New Thought movement said, "Let us convert prayer into a conscious communion with the Invisible," meaning having faith in a God who is present becomes a dynamic use of our spiritual power. Gone are the days God sits in judgment of our worthiness to receive our good. Instead prayers that affirm an open, creative channel for God's greater ideas to flow through us emphasize more about what is right with us than what is wrong. Positive statements connected to heart-felt words, and spoken with faith and an attitude of gratitude, are affirmative prayers. Dr. Barker stated it another way: "The direction of your language indicates the direction of your thinking." (*Barkerisms,* p.44; also see Treatment on p. 16 of this workbook.)

Awakened thinkers: Awakened thinkers, as taught by Dr. Barker, are individuals unafraid of spiritual ideas, who instead welcome and analyze them to find their creativeness and personal application [creating demonstrations.] Awakened thinkers seek better ideas to produce better results and solve the problems that confront them today. Progressive thinking is activated by the word yes and never the word no, which means all thought is a forward moving action to realize some desired good in the future.

Barkerisms: These are exceptional, potent statements used frequently by Dr. Barker. They were so popular they eventually became known as "Barkerisms" and were popularized in all his lectures and books. These Barkerisms will be sprinkled like diamonds throughout this workbook, each one carefully selected to illuminate and increase the reader's reflection and understanding of important ideas and concepts. Each Barkerism adds warmth and color, inviting all readers to adopt its use. Dr. Barker said that a Barkerism was "to be contemplated in order to draw from it an essence which will inspire you to further creative thinking." (p.3) Here are a couple of examples of Barkerisms: "An expanded experience will never happen until an expanded consciousness precedes it." (p.18) "Everything that is wrong with you is a conditioning of the past. And everything that is right with you is a potential of the future." (p.5)

Consciousness: Dr. Barker said our experiences can first be explained by what we have thought with our conscious mind. This interaction between what we think [personal awareness] and the subconscious level [thoughts of God] determines our experience. Once a decision is made your subconscious goes to work on your demonstration – your thoughts are always in the process of becoming things.

Decision: The most important function of the individual mind is a decision to make up one's mind. It is a commitment to a course of action after some consideration: an intention to create.

Demonstrations: Both good and bad ideas require thoughts to put them into action. Though we don't plan it, bad ideas can become our focus and hold our attention for long periods. Think of some great ideas like the invention of the mobile phone or Facebook; both were made real by the persistent thought and talented efforts of their creators. By a similar examination of the facts and events of your own life, you too can learn to see how your thought patterns and ideas led you to the choices you've made: the spouse you chose, the profession you entered, the college you attended, or the home you chose, for example. Each historical action you undertook came from a single, powerful idea that lead to a meaningful outcome called a demonstration, a result made real, good or bad. Unless you assess how you got there, you may not be aware of how powerful your thoughts and emotions are in making your decisions. Each of your intended or unintended results in life [those made real] are proof of sustained mental effort. These are ideas coming forth from your subconscious mind in order to bring about something in your experience that you desire. (Also see **Law of Growth** on p.13 and **Subconscious Mind** on p.15 of this workbook.)

First Cause: Can you accept a loving God, the First Cause behind all creation, is ready to make your ideas real? Can you believe this to be true? You can know God first hand, personal and up close by believing everything around you is intelligence, God in action, or what Dr. Barker called our opportunity to receive our "Divine Bounty." How can we connect with an intelligence that is innate and intuitive? First, we need to call it what it is: our birthright! Accept it. Recognize that our ideas come to us from God as we consciously recognize some good we want for ourselves. Secondly, we, the Spirit within us, must make a decision to act, accepting some good for ourselves. Perfect ideas come to us from God [intelligence made ready for our use] to create specific demonstrations we want and desire. Third, we express a level of expectancy, believing we will experience these desires of the heart, and at the expense of no other person. (Also see **Universal Intelligence** and **Universal Mind** on p.18 of this workbook.)

Intelligence: "Everything is intelligence and the Principle of intelligence is responsiveness. Therefore the person making a decision is using their intelligence to evoke a responsiveness on the part of a greater Intelligence to have their decision fulfilled," explains Rev. Dr. Lloyd George Tupper, teacher of spiritual principles and New Thought Minister. In *The Power of Decision*, Dr. Barker always emphasized we are here [on earth] to use our conscious mind to select all the greater ideas God has for us. Dr. Ernest Holmes, Founder of Religious Science and another New Thought leader in the 20th century, explained as individuals we have a higher form of intelligence and as such more volition to choose what we want and think. As such, a higher form of intelligence places less restriction on our use of it. He went on to say, "Matter has form; intelligence has thought," and as such matter [form] always has restrictions or limitations while our thought is never limited. (Also see **Universal Mind** on p.18 of this workbook.)

Intuition: "What is intuition? A clear knowing without being able to explain how one knows, or knowledge gained without logical or rational thought. Intuition is receipt of information from a nonphysical database." (*The Intuitive Healer* by Marcia Emery, Ph.D, p. 5)

Law of Growth: You can accelerate the Law of Growth, but you cannot bypass it. Every person is like the seedling in the window box; neither the plant nor the person can fight the earth, the sun, or the rain. Instead, we must use them for our needs. In turn, as our ideas about the world around us mature, our consciousness grows and unfolds according to this law (*Barkerisms*). At times, our results [demonstrations] appear miraculous. Without understanding that the Law of Growth is at work in our lives, we declare, "It's a miracle!" Although miracles appear to escape the Law of Growth, this conclusion is entirely in error. Our receptive state of consciousness evolves as new ideas are acted on and we begin to achieve our goals. But in most instances, we are entirely unaware of what God is or is doing in our lives. As we can't escape the Law of Gravity, we cannot escape being fundamentally intertwined with the Law of Growth. God, however, is not subject to the Law of Gravity, but we are. All ideas come from God, so it is best to keep our expectations focused on God's influence at work in our lives. Too often, our expectations go unmet if left in the hands of other people. We should direct our expectations to God alone; it is here all expectations will be met, or often exceeded. That's the miracle in effect. The Law of Growth acts upon all people, just as it acts upon all seeds cast into the soil. It does not choose to act on one seed alone. It acts equally on all seeds just as it acts on all individuals. The Law of Growth must act intelligently. Even if it takes your inferior idea to its logical end [your demonstration], it won't argue with you. Neither does the Law of Growth pass judgment on your decisions. The Law only carries them out, just as it brings plants to maturity from the soil. As no one escapes the Law of Growth, a healthy respect for the Law at work in your life is prudent.

Your results will be produced with the same vitality as found in all of nature. However, your cooperation could enhance your demonstration. (Also see **Demonstrations** on p.11 and **Treatment** on p.16 of this workbook.)

Law of Mind: Your most priceless possession is your mind, and what you are doing with it at this instant is significant. Mind [Law of Mind] is invisible, but its activity in you [your demonstrations] is visible to all who know you. Refer to Dr. Barker's book, *You Are Invisible: No One Has Seen Your Consciousness.* Your individual mind is the key to all your experience. Whether you think BIG or small makes all the difference in your demonstrations. Some call it a "God Mind," which is meant to be expressed in you, as you. You individualize your demonstrations using the Law of Mind. It is always enabling you to express your ideas of health, creativity, and prosperous living, whether BIG or small in each outcome. The greater Mind of God conceived you as a perfect idea and endowed you with all the intelligence necessary to unfold a greater idea of yourself. Use as little or as much of this intelligence as you desire. Only ignorance of the Law of Mind and an inferior decision made by you can place a limit on your potential.

Modern Definition of God: Dr. Barker said all creation comes from one Creative Intelligence creating out of itself, which means God is infinite in its intelligence and operates in an infinite field of emotion [your mind]. God is always present in all matters of life. God creates out of itself with omniscient purpose and precise action.

New Thought: Dr. Barker believed that "religious systems have taught doctrines of repression," rather than focusing on our spiritual desires to know God. Dr. Barker saw New Thought as a universal pathway for all seekers, regardless of background. He wanted everyone to experience a "divinely balanced process of creative consciousness" with a loving God. New Thought taught God's greater ideas were to be discovered. God as the source of all intelligence becomes a universal well-spring for greater love, health, abundance and creativity while living here on earth. Gone are the days of a God absent in our present circumstances, sitting somewhere on a throne judging our worthiness to receive answers to our prayers.

New Thought came out of a revival of spirituality in the mid-1850's in America and ushered in affirmative prayer known as Spiritual Mind Healing, a method of prayer emphasizing the spiritual perfection of each individual. This method of scientific or affirmative prayer continues to be practiced by many groups in the United States and abroad. New Thought was formalized under three historic denominations: Religious Science founded by Dr. Ernest Holmes, Unity School of Christianity founded by Charles and Myrtle Fillmore, and Christian Science founded by Mary Baker Eddy.

Spiritual Evolution: In *The Science of Successful Living: Your Spiritual Formula for A Joyous Life*, Dr. Barker states, "Spiritual evolution is yours for the taking. It requires your decision, your willingness to let go of present comfort [complacency] and launch out into paths of new trials (new ideas) with their inevitable good results [demonstrations]. To do this you cease from condemning your human mind and its mistakes … the whole creative process is in your mind and heart awaiting your acknowledgment." (p. 24)

Subconscious Mind: Your subconscious mind is often referred to as your SOUL and is the major creative operation of your life, including your entire physical body. It is demonstrated in how alert, responsive, or aware you are: the sensitivity with which you react. Your subconscious is a subjective mind; it must go to work for you at the instant you make a decision. The quality of its demonstration relies upon your own evolved state of consciousness. The subjective mind is entirely creative but also impersonal. You might call it the silent builder in your life, and it is responsible for sustaining your body as well as health. This subjective mind assumes any role you give it. Of great importance to remember is whatever you think in your subjective mind will become your experience. Its role is to act upon everything you think as if it were true; it cannot deny, argue, or reject what you put into your thoughts; that is why it is subjective. You might think of it as your "inner mind" while your conscious thought is your "outer mind" that you think with daily. Dr. Barker says that your subconscious mind is really "your best friend, your creator, your ally" and as such should be trusted implicitly. This subjective mind is part of the Universal Mind [of God] while your subconscious mind is an individualization of that one Mind. Since the subjective mind is receptive to all your thinking, ask yourself, "What am I thinking right now?" Upon reflection, you might also stand back and look at your thoughts a little more objectively, weighing in on the emotional tone and mood they hold as well. (Also see **Law of Growth** on p. 13 and **Universal Mind** on p. 18 of this workbook.)

Treatment: When asked what Spiritual Mind Treatment was, Dr. Barker stated, "I define it as using your conscious mind to select what you want, and next directing your subconscious mind to bring this [perfect result] into objective experiences [demonstrations.] (Barker, *Treat Yourself to Life*, p. 6) Other religions and spiritual circles may call it affirmative prayer. However, Dr. Barker wanted to explain there was a difference. Treatment is the science of inducing with your mind a concept or an idea for greater living. It's not about focusing on things. Traditional prayer often says you need to plead for something or offer a grievance why you didn't get something. Realize when you speak a Treatment you need an idea or a concept, not a list of requested items. Learn that the entire action of receiving your good is a mental action. You are the thinker; a perceiver of concepts and ideas God is offering you. Whatever of these you choose to focus on in your Treatment determines what your experiences will be in the world. In other words, your goal is the correct perception of what God wants for you. So, when you realize you have an incorrect perception or inferior thought, give yourself a Treatment through this scientific method explained later.

Spiritual Mind Treatment is an affirmative step-by-step form of prayer given to the world by Dr. Ernest Holmes, a great philosopher and spiritual genius. He discovered a method of prayer thought to be used by Jesus and taught the five steps of Treatment to all of his audiences around the world. His discovery came after spending years distilling the great truths of philosophy, theology, and psychology, as well as the basic principles of science related to energy, matter, and

form, melding them all into one practical way to get better results. His commitment to this form of prayer was so strong, he trained and certified what he designated as Practitioners to be the healing arm for all churches, known today as Centers For Spiritual Living. He also required all Ministers to become proficient in Spiritual Mind Treatments, using this form of prayer in all services and classes. Centers all over the world use affirmative prayer they call "Treatments" to reveal the perfection of the physical body as well as for the mind to be open to acceptance of a loving God that is never reluctant to help. Dr. Holmes and his Practitioners and Ministers alike all made it their mission to help people discover a more affirmative way to pray where God's ideas for the highest and best use by the person are meant to be realized to improve one's circumstances, including health and well-being. In a Treatment, God is not being asked to give people things, but to deliver ideas to them that help them overcome any condition or circumstance. The popularity of the spiritual wisdom of Dr. Holmes and his Ministers, among them Dr. Raymond Charles Barker, formerly a Unity Minister, allowed them to travel widely throughout the United States, Europe, and elsewhere to educate churches, businesses professional organizations, large corporations, community, and interfaith groups about New Thought as an affirmative form of spirituality and healing through Treatments. Many of the basic tenants, principles, and concepts founded by these early pioneers of New Thought ministries, like the one Dr. Holmes created, are used widely today in personal development, coaching practices, and self-discovery programs. A Treatment openly affirms God is never withholding Its WILLINGNESS TO SERVE. Treatment is never applied to a reluctant God but is an open recognition of what God IS and is willing TO DO in the life of both the person speaking the Treatment as well as the person receiving the Treatment. Each time a Treatment is done, any individual person is believed to fully experience the highest qualities of God by being one with the Mind of God. Every person can have the experience of their own perfection revealed through this affirmative form of prayer. (Also see Demonstrations, p.11, Law of Growth, p.13, Universal Mind, p.18, **and a Special Section on How to Give Yourself a Spiritual Mind Treatment in Five Proven Steps on p.181 in this workbook.**

Universal Intelligence: Dr. Barker believed that the universe is a creative intelligence acting continuously and producing an orderly outcome through the Law of Growth; this is what produces our demonstrations here on earth. Dr. Barker believed that each person is intimately connected to this constant intelligent, creative action. He frequently referred to Universal Intelligence as Mind [God], and always emphasized its importance by using a capital "M" in his writings.

Universal Mind: We coexist with Universal Mind, connecting to it through our individual, subconscious mind; it's our portal to God [all Intelligence]. Dr. Ernest Holmes best described it as Intelligence with a capital "I" or Spirit with a capital "S." Either way you wish to express it, it is God in action in your life. Scientific exploration has proven the cosmos is no longer a universe but rather a multiverse of abundant, intelligent matter. And to this end, God is also responding to us and always working through us with Its greater intelligence, though sometimes we can be unresponsive or even in denial of God's influence at times. This is when we make erroneous decisions. These are the times when we hold onto an inferior thought or belief. As we evolve in our own state of consciousness by accepting better ideas, we open ourselves up to a greater use of this unlimited Intelligence. God, as you have learned, does not give us things, but rather gives us intelligent ideas to advance all our goals. Mistakenly we can dispose of those ideas by ignoring them or replacing them with something we feel works much better – our willpower and inferior thoughts often formed through prior experiences. But if we accept God has better ideas for us, this profound Intelligence walks alongside us down a trail of successes that show we have been intelligent and responsive to God's presence throughout our lives. God's ideas are the only true power behind all our decisions once we commit ourselves to more beneficial outcomes. Within this Universal Mind [which is the broadest possible potential given to all of us by God] we can experience the individual perfection found in all of us. (Also see Intelligence on p. 12 and Subconscious Mind on p. 15 of this workbook.)

What Could Be Holding Me Back?

Inferior Thoughts

Dr. Barker said to make yours the open mind, the navigable channel for great ideas, which means your personal self-expression of love, health, and wealth comes at the cost of giving up negative-prone ways of thinking that block your path. He reminded us an open mind also underscores our willingness to become flexible.

What Do I Believe?

STEP 1

Answer Five Questions to Start Your Journey

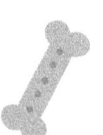

1

Do I believe a healthy mind is my natural birthright?

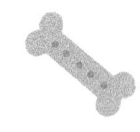

2

Do I believe I have the power to change what is in my consciousness?

3

Do I believe cloudy thoughts can delay the process of making a good decision?

4

Do I believe my problems are not in my life to improve me?

5

Do I believe my fears and doubts can hold me back?

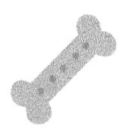

Workbook Chapter Summary

Barker wrote about the **Letter of the Law** in his book *The Power of Decision*, a book with many great insights. But not until the *Power Your Decisions Self-Study Workbook* was published did new audiences experience the **Spirit of the Law – the practical steps to making better decisions.** This self-study uses contemporary language to explain difficult concepts and a vocabulary you can apply immediately, offering multiple illustrations to help you walk the talk of these 20th century giants. You will soon recognize how inferior thoughts, outdated beliefs, and habits are placing great limitations on your results. Read everything that has been prepared for your journey with an open mind. Work your exercises with care and great thought. You will soon discover what is valuable to your understanding. Let's get started!

One new idea can guide you to better results. These ideas are earmarked for you from birth. Each idea will come to you with all the provisions necessary to help you succeed. Most people don't make this self-discovery until late in life, if at all. This is simple in concept but not always easy to practice. To begin to receive your greatest ideas, accept yourself as being an individualized version of Universal Mind: y-o-u a-r-e i-t! Successful people all over the world use the same Universal Mind in every field of endeavor. Geniuses are not born; instead, they know intuitively how to express their genius in the same way you can. Their ideas were revealed early in life because they didn't resist them; they explored them instead. They started early in life through a practical and dedicated application of their ideas to some endeavor. But it's not too late for you. You too can find your own genius. You will soon learn how to prepare your mind daily to access this same Universal Mind through Spiritual Mind Treatment. Prepare yourself to fill your own pipeline with intelligent ideas and better results. You will be given more instruction on this in Chapter 4.

Unfortunately, most people are entirely unaware that they use the same old thinking. They can often believe in bad luck or explain to others their life circumstances are due to someone else's negligence.

These misdirected thoughts cause disruptions of all kinds. It's here inferior thinking creates casualties in careers, relationships, health, and creative endeavors. Even worse, most unintelligent thoughts or "inferior" thoughts live on through a power of the will. Held long enough, they become expectations that disappoint us. If left unchecked and unexamined, these thoughts lead to a cycle of poverty thinking.

Barkerisms
to Take Into Your Everyday Life

Any thinking that is backed up with an emotional intent (good or bad) will get results.

Every basic habit pattern that is constructive is an orderly one. It is wise to have them. We have to have them in order to function.

Poverty thinking is a belief that the good you are seeking is leaving you.

Poverty thinking also convinces you that your good is being withheld, perhaps by your circumstances at birth, or because of some misfortune beyond your control. Poverty is a powerful thought, but so too is prosperity. Are you thinking poor health is normal for your age? Is there a temptation for substance abuse typical for someone with your family history? Have you felt unworthy because a particular circumstance lead you to a feeling of resignation?

Your workbook is now your roadmap to show you your mind is your greatest asset! You can change your circumstances and recover from past decisions once you learn how to accept a new and better idea about yourself. Allow these better thoughts to improve your experiences. This doesn't take time as much as it takes practice. Using the right tools helps you get into the right frame of mind. That's how this all works together as a guided experience to put you on a new pathway to better results. So Barky asks: "Are you ready to let go of unexamined thoughts?"

Words, Concepts, and Phrases
You Will Need to Practice in Chapter One

In a few simple words, write out what each vocabulary word means. Refer to page 10, the vocabulary section, to review and think about what you understand about each definition. The vocabulary has been written carefully and thoughtfully to help you understand spiritual terms, concepts, and practices. A new vocabulary is essential to help you deepen your understanding about what is powering your decision to bring about your desired result. Once you better understand these words and how to use them correctly, you will grow into a more evolved spiritual thinker who gets better results.

First Cause:

_____
_____
_____
_____
_____
_____
_____

Law of Mind:

_____
_____
_____
_____
_____
_____
_____

Intelligence:

_____
_____
_____
_____
_____
_____

Subconscious Mind:

_____
_____
_____
_____
_____
_____

Universal Intelligence:

_____
_____
_____
_____
_____
_____

Universal Mind:

_____
_____
_____
_____
_____
_____

Quizzical Barky Says It's Time to Journal Your Impressions

Dig a little deeper into what is in your mind!

Writing contributes to emotional well-being, increases mental and emotional clarity, reduces stress, and increases problem-solving.

Write down your AH-HA moments, realizations, recognitions, or exclamations of sudden understanding. For example, did any of the five questions cause you to stop and ponder your answers? Did you think back on a specific life choice you made? Did the chapter summary make you think more deeply about a personal goal or decision? Are you considering how you might grow more spiritual? Perhaps one or more AH-HA moments include all of the above! ***What has been stirred up inside of you? Write your impressions down here.***

_____

_____

_____

_____

_____

_____

_____

_____

_____

_____

_____

_____

_____

_____

Personalized Workbook Exercises

EXERCISE ONE

Everyone desires to express themselves intelligently in all of the following **life areas:**

- **Health**
- **Wealth / Money**
- **Joy**
- **Self-expression/Evolving**
- **Career/Avocation**
- **Love**

Inferior thinking sometimes ties our mental energy into negative knots. It starts with these:

- **Worry**
- **Fear**
- **Dis-ease**
- **Envy**
- **Hate**
- **Resentment**
- **Argument**

What's in your Mind?

Are you experiencing any areas of your life where inferior thinking has shown up? These feelings or moods may be blocking your growth and holding you back. Write out your answers on the next three pages.

Examples about health:

Worry · *Fear* · *Dis-ease* · *Resentment* · *Envy* · *Argument* · *Hate*

HEALTH
What's in your Mind?

I worry *about a loss of memory as I grow older.*

I fear *I am taking too much medicine for my good.*

I resent *that I did not take better care of my skin earlier in life.*

I feel dis-ease *in my life is going to require a counselor to help me.*

I am envious *of others who've never had a sick day in their life!*

I hate *to think I am just another statistic after my diagnosis.*

I argue *with myself all the time I should lose weight.*

What inferior thoughts or beliefs do I have about my health?

I worry _____

_____

I fear _____

_____

I resent_____

_____

I expect disease _____

I am envious _____

I hate _____

I argue _____

HEALTH
What's in your Mind?

Worry • Fear • Dis-ease • Resentment • Envy • Hate • Argument

What keeps me raising the alarm bells over money?

I worry _____

_____

I fear _____

_____

I resent _____

_____

I expect disease _____

I am envious _____

I hate _____

I argue _____

MONEY
What's in your Mind?

Worry • Fear • Dis-ease • Resentment • Envy • Hate • Argument

What is placing limits on my joy?

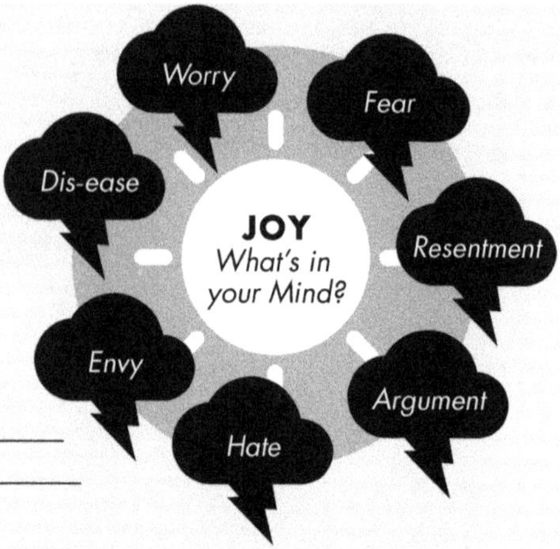

I worry _____
_____

I fear _____
_____

I resent _____
_____

I expect disease _____

I am envious _____

I hate _____

I argue _____

Worry

Fear

Dis-ease

JOY
What's in your Mind?

Resentment

Envy

Argument

Hate

What keeps me from evolving? Why do I resist change?

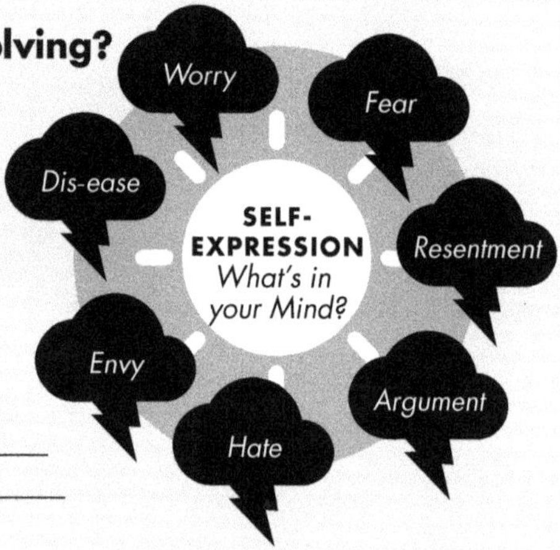

I worry_____
_____

I fear _____
_____

I resent _____
_____

I expect disease _____

I am envious _____

I hate _____

I argue _____

Worry

Fear

Dis-ease

SELF-EXPRESSION
What's in your Mind?

Resentment

Envy

Argument

Hate

What stands between me and feeling successful?

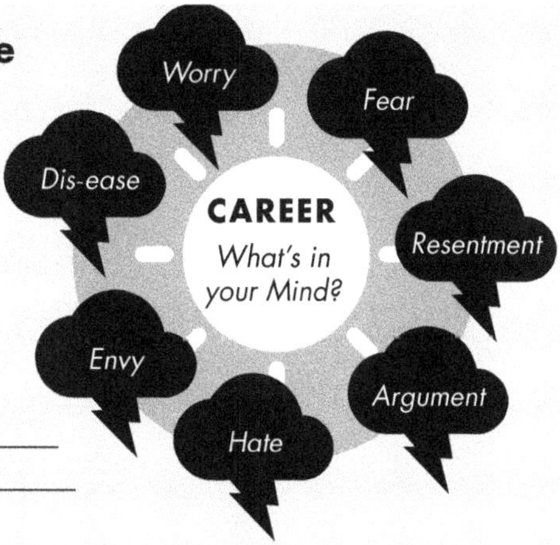

I worry _____
_____

I fear _____
_____

I resent _____
_____

I expect disease _____

I am envious _____

I hate _____

I argue _____

Worry

Fear

Dis-ease

CAREER
*What's in
your Mind?*

Resentment

Envy

Argument

Hate

What holds me back from expressing what I love or who I love?

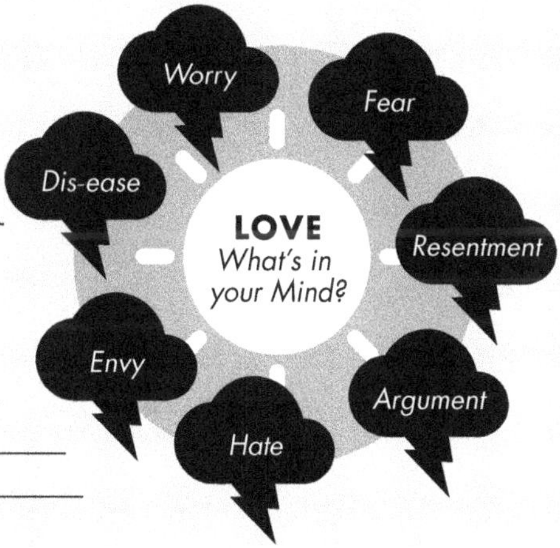

I worry _____
_____

I fear _____
_____

I resent _____
_____

I expect disease _____

I am envious _____

I hate _____

I argue _____

Worry

Fear

Dis-ease

LOVE
*What's in
your Mind?*

Resentment

Envy

Argument

Hate

29

EXERCISE TWO

First: After completing Exercise One, what are you capable of changing right now in your life? What do you have control over?

Second: Rank your next steps you can initiate today. List from 1 to 6, with 1 being the most urgent to do and 6 being of lesser importance. Think deeply before you prioritize. If you found no life area you want to improve, leave it blank, but feel free to contribute to a list of next steps in other areas to keep a history of next steps.

Examples of next steps to improve health: RANK

- *Start walking 30 minutes everyday* ⬚ 3

- *Explore my options with holistic doctors* ⬚ 4

- *Change my diet to include more nutritious foods* ⬚ 1

- *See a dermatologist about a skincare plan* ⬚ 6

- *Follow-up on a sleep study my doctor offered* ⬚ 5

- *Reorganize some personal space in my home for quiet meditation* ⬚ 2

Next steps to improve my health RANK

- _____ ☐

- _____ ☐

- _____ ☐

- _____ ☐

- _____ ☐

- _____ ☐

Next steps to improve my relationship with money

RANK

- _____ ☐
- _____ ☐
- _____ ☐
- _____ ☐
- _____ ☐
- _____ ☐

Next steps to increase my joy

RANK

- _____ ☐
- _____ ☐
- _____ ☐
- _____ ☐
- _____ ☐
- _____ ☐

Next steps to expand my creative self-expression

RANK

- _____ ☐
- _____ ☐
- _____ ☐
- _____ ☐
- _____ ☐
- _____ ☐

Next steps to advance my career or avocational interests

RANK

- _____ ☐
- _____ ☐
- _____ ☐
- _____ ☐
- _____ ☐
- _____ ☐

Next steps to express more love in my life

RANK

- _____ ☐
- _____ ☐
- _____ ☐
- _____ ☐
- _____ ☐
- _____ ☐

Next steps to open other new doors in my life

RANK

- _____ ☐
- _____ ☐
- _____ ☐
- _____ ☐
- _____ ☐
- _____ ☐

EXERCISE THREE

Make a list of the #1 areas that you would most like to feel better about.

Now that you have written down a variety of next steps for those life areas you are focused on, pick your top three (3) you most want to complete. Here are some examples to think about.

Example: (My #1 top areas of concern)

Where I routinely focus my thoughts, emotions, and expectations:

How I am going to improve my health:
RANK

1. Change my diet to include more nutritious foods.

2. Reorganize some personal space for quiet meditation.

3. Start walking 30 minutes each day.

How I am going to improve my career / avocational interests:
RANK

1. Get an appointment for career counseling to find my strengths.

2. See what paid options for education I have through my current work.

3. Return to taking classes to finish my degree.

How I am going to improve my relationship to money:
RANK

1. Stop believing my only options are low-paying jobs.

2. Set up an in-person appointment with a financial advisor and open an account.

3. Stop spending frivolously and cut down on my use of credit cards.

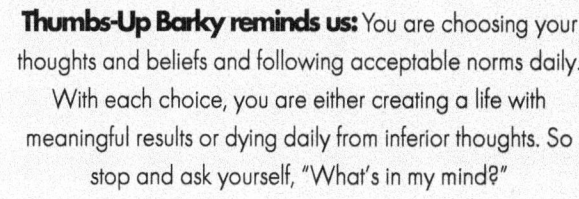

Thumbs-Up Barky reminds us: You are choosing your thoughts and beliefs and following acceptable norms daily. With each choice, you are either creating a life with meaningful results or dying daily from inferior thoughts. So stop and ask yourself, "What's in my mind?"

Now is your turn to summarize your top next steps! Write down your highest priority next steps for up to three areas of your life:

LIFE AREA #1: _____

Rank   **Top next steps for me to see a breakthrough**

☐   _____

☐   _____

☐   _____

LIFE AREA #2 _____

Rank   **Top next steps for me to see a breakthrough**

☐   _____

☐   _____

☐   _____

LIFE AREA #3 _____

Rank   **Top next steps for me to see a breakthrough**

☐   _____

☐   _____

☐   _____

You will discover, after several weeks of study, you may want
to change or revise what you wrote down in these Chapter One
exercises. This is natural to reassess your priorities. It may take you
several attempts to raise your awareness of what's important to
you. That gnawing sense that something is holding you back or
stifling your potential must be brought to an honest and open level
of personal awareness.

Assess if you are ready to make these changes in your life!

Personal growth may often require a personal assessment of your habits of thought and emotions. Now is a great time to assess the depth of your personal self-awareness, motivation, and willingness to grow emotionally and evolve in your decision-making.

Now is a great time to ask yourself this compelling question: "Am I ready to accept more of everything in my life, more love, health, joy, happiness, and a greater self-expression of myself?" Do you have the willingness to venture on to get this question answered? If you are, turn now to a Special Section for Practical Help on page 162 to assess your readiness.

POINTER BARKY SAYS GO TO PAGE 162 NOW!

Takeaways to Raise My Consciousness

A Review of Chapter One

We are all residents in the continuous creation of the Universe. Everyone is given the mental and spiritual equipment to live effectively. The operating instructions to live a happier life are simple: you have to work mentally and emotionally in sync with the Intelligence of the Universal Mind. This is the beginning of how to think c-o-r-r-e-c-t-l-y.

Add these new enriched ways of thinking to your day:

- All the resources to fulfill your greatest ideas are already yours. Each idea needs you for its perfect self-expression.

- Letting go of an old notion that has completed its course in your experience is more important than the decision to welcome a new idea.

- The word *no* has tremendous power. What you mentally say *no* to will soon depart from your life.

- Thinking and feeling negative over a period of time will not bring about positive situations in your experience.

- You were born to unfold, evolve, and create as a responsive and intelligent thinker.

- Indecision is a decision to fail.

- Problems result from unintelligent thinking. A Universal Intelligence must assume that what you are thinking is really what you want to have as your experience in life.

- A new train of ideas is the beginning of a cure to all your problems.

- Always search out new ideas that fascinate you. Great ideas are meant to make you happier, more prosperous, healthier, and more loving.

- Realize that you individualize a wealth of possibilities. You can be what you want and have what you want when you align your thoughts with Universal Intelligence.

- You were meant to live in these times and are equipped to meet any challenge. Be the breakthrough thinker you were born to be.

- You are the right person in the right place at the right time to create the perfect world for yourself.

Happy Barky wants you to run, not walk, to your future success!

"Make up your mind to devote one week solely to the task of building a new habit of thought, and during that week let everything in life be unimportant as compared to that. If you will do so, then that week will be the most significant week in your whole life. It will literally be the turning point for you. If you will do so, it is safe to say your whole life will change for the better. In fact, nothing can possibly remain the same."

Emmet Fox, *The 7-Day Mental Diet*, p. 9

Am I Stuck in a Cycle of Worry?

Failing to Decide

Dr. Barker reminded us our mind and
our emotions are the only real tools in life
we can depend upon.

Ask Yourself: What Do I Believe?

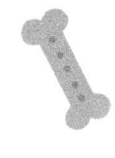

Answer Five Questions to Start Your Journey

Do I believe it takes as much mental work to be a failure as it does to be a success?

Do I believe my circumstances reflect how I have handled things emotionally in my life?

Do I believe some of my lost opportunities came because I investigated all the probable reasons why something could not succeed?

Do I believe there were delays in my results because I worried too much at times?

Do I believe original thinking could have gotten me better results in one area of my life?

Workbook Chapter Summary

 orry and indecision go together. Ask yourself: what keeps you wringing your hands and pacing the floor at night? It's worry! And how has worry served you? It hasn't. It has led to a lot of wasted energy that could have been used productively. Dr. Barker believed worry began as a childhood pattern of indecision and left unchecked became an ingrained habit in adulthood.

Barkerisms
to Take Into Your Everyday Life

Fear, worry, and other negative thinking caused by your indecisiveness are like silt gradually collecting in a navigable river.

An expanded experience will never happen until an expanded consciousness precedes it.

A decision to stop all worry is a decision to return all power back to you. This was Dr. Barker's mantra. No adult person benefits from a choice that someone else makes for them; it underscores that a person is incapable of making their own decisions. Another way to say this is that worriers automatically hold off from making their own decisions. They run in place by putting one foot on the brake while pressing on the gas with the other. In the end they create a lot of noise and smoke and wear out a good set of nerves. Worriers should stop betting someone else can do a better job running their lives.

Indecision is a personal decision to fail.

The success process is simple and direct: know you have within your mind the best ideas for each right decision for you. Each idea will occur at the right time and in the proper sequence through a Law of Growth. But first you must accept an eternal truth: an intelligent and creative Universe must work through you. There is no strain or stress to express this Universal Intelligence: just simply be yourself. However, many people simply choose not to express their intelligence and make no decision. This keeps success at bay. The more they focus their worry on conditions, the more confused thinking is fostered within. An evolved consciousness stops this negative loop of frustrated thinking.

Barkerisms
*to Take Into Your
Everyday Life*

Start clearing the now in order to have what you want in the future.

No one has ever gone forward by looking backward.

Dr. Barker explains how this loop begins in the subconscious. The subconscious is your spiritual well, a place where God and your thoughts coexist. Your subconscious has a unique feature: it can never argue or debate the thoughts you give it. No matter how confused your thoughts or poorly constructed your idea, the subconscious cannot argue with you and tell you that you are about to make a big mistake. It only knows to obey your thought and direction.

Through a Law of Growth, a thought you hold long enough [with feeling and passion] will be acted upon. The Law of Growth acts on your thoughts [ideas] leading to all your results [demonstrations], delivered on time and in perfect order for your situation. Remember, each idea comes with all the provisions necessary for its fulfillment. Dr. Barker illustrated this poignant process and showed you how our inferior thinking shows up. Unless you pluck out an inferior thought, it will show up in your results again and again, only clothed in different circumstances, geographic locations, and relationships.

Your subconscious is a thought-activated system. While a GPS system navigates a clear, direct pathway to your destination, your subconscious navigates with only your thoughts as information. Give it good information and you get better results; it's that simple. Always examine your motivation, goals, and needs before you leap. This is so essential, as relying on routine thoughts and unchallenged, inferior ways of thinking can only lead to unchanged results. You may find yourself right back where you started, but with a different spouse, a different job, or a more serious health issue. Only years later does it become clear to you that your previous thoughts and expectations, some of them inferior, have gone unchallenged.

New Thought practitioners like Dr. Barker believed that situations, events, and even things come into our lives from ideas we accepted about ourselves long ago. People often assess these results from a superficial understanding, even blaming others. Only what they see, hear, or feel in the moment counts. Making observations on these surface facts alone may allow inferior thoughts to remain undisturbed below the surface for years. Dr. Barker explained that these external or superficial facts often betray internal moods and feelings. The real cause of inferior thinking may be buried beneath layers of hurt and confused thoughts about ourselves that accumulate over the years. Unless we stop this cycle of inferior thinking, our problems won't go away; they fester and get worse.

The subconscious mind does not procrastinate.

A successful identification of our exposed, personal problems presses us to look within. Intuition can often be a useful tool to see ourselves more clearly. Intuition urges us to open up to greater self-exploration; it's here God's better ideas are waiting for us. But first, we must consciously accept them and claim them as our own! When we understand our demonstrations [results in life] are our own fulfilled thoughts, we can ask ourselves, "Did I use the right idea and motivation to make that last important decision?" Asking God for more intelligent ideas to guide you to better results can start a daily, conscious cycle of spiritual thinking. Freedom from all inferior thoughts and emotions can be yours when you understand how your mind works. As an individualized personality and expression of God, you co-create with the intelligence of Universal Mind. What could be more intelligent than accepting the brilliance of the Universal Mind as your own?

In Dr. Barker's success process [a process of growing spiritually], you maintain your conviction that healthy ideas are your greatest asset. Through an expanded consciousness, new thoughts pave the way to new decisions. All that is required of you is to consciously and deliberately cultivate these new ideas as your own. Dr. Barker called this intelligence your "inheritance incorruptible" as mentioned in the Bible. He also said that anything that has occurred in your past puts no limitations on your future. A new idea about yourself today can take you in an entirely new direction tomorrow, if you allow it. But before a real change can occur, spiritual thinking must take root. As you are finding in this workbook, now is the right time to release inferior thoughts that are holding you back.

Barkerisms
to Take Into Your Everyday Life

Many people fall into the trap of thinking that life is a struggle. When they believe this, they are on the road to failure.

You do not store up goodness. You maintain goodness by remaining good, and your constant flow of right thought is the answer to everything.

Unintelligent thoughts only delay your good. And indecision will certainly guarantee it. A failure-prone person seeks to void out the positives in their mind. Any positive thought can turn that around. Allow many positive ideas to flow into your thinking as you read this workbook and do your exercises. Dr. Barker tells us to accept these truths about ourselves. Again and again, he counsels us to remember that our only tools in life are our mind and emotions. Accept his wise words; you too can begin to wisely choose each and every right idea that comes your way.

"We don't see things as they are; we see things as we are."

Anais Nin, essayist

Words, Concepts, and Phrases to Practice in Chapter Two

In a few simple words, write out what each vocabulary word means. Refer to page 10, the vocabulary section, to review and think about what you understand about each definition. The vocabulary has been written carefully and thoughtfully to help you understand spiritual terms, concepts, and practices. A new vocabulary is essential to help you deepen your understanding about what is powering your decision to bring about your desired result. Once you better understand these words and how to use them correctly, you will grow into a more evolved spiritual thinker who gets better results.

Awakened Thinkers:

_____
_____
_____
_____
_____
_____

Barkerisms:

_____
_____
_____
_____
_____
_____

Consciousness:

_____
_____
_____
_____
_____
_____

Subconscious Mind:

_____
_____
_____
_____
_____
_____

"Over 90% of all neural processing and 95% of decision-making is being made by your non-conscious brain. Despite how it might feel, most of your perceptions, experiences, decisions, and conclusions are made at the subconscious level, fed to the conscious brain, and mediated by the social, emotional, biological parts of your brain."

Brynn Winegard, Ph.D.,

from the keynote "Secrets of Success"

www.drbrynn.com

Baby Barky Says It's Time to Journal Your Impressions

Baby steps will help you look before you leap!

Writing contributes to emotional well-being, increases mental and emotional clarity, reduces stress, and increases problem-solving.

Write down your AH-HA moments, realizations, recognitions, or exclamations of sudden understanding. For example, did any of the five questions cause you to stop and ponder your answers? Did you think back on a specific life choice you made? Did the chapter summary make you think more deeply about a personal goal or decision? Are you considering how you might grow more spiritual? Perhaps one or more AH-HA moments include all of the above! *What has been stirred up inside of you? Write your impressions down here.*

_____

_____

_____

_____

_____

_____

_____

_____

_____

_____

_____

_____

_____

_____

_____

_____

_____

_____

Dr. Barker said that he was amazed that everyone is not seeking all the greatness that can be known, thought, or experienced. Goodness, he explains, comes with sound contemplation and can be experienced by every person who seeks it.

Barky says don't expect miracles but do expect the miraculous!

This cosmic process is not an ancient one but is a correct way of thinking both universally and individually. What God does on a grand scale across the cosmos you can do on this earthly plane. Successful people may never realize they are using a spiritual means to achieve their goals, but they are. You can too! This is the only success process you will ever need. Know what you want, make a decision that it can happen for you, and act upon every idea that comes to you to make your dream come true. Your subconscious mind is your natural tool to help you realize all your decisions. **It never procrastinates to get the job done you've asked it to.**

Personalized Workbook Exercises

EXERCISE ONE

Now that you have clarified the life areas you most want to work on in your Chapter One exercises, let's see if indecision has also become a problem. Sometimes we are unaware we STOP or PROLONG getting a result out of fear or self-doubt. These among other inferior thoughts cause us not to make our decisions when we need to.

So, could indecision be keeping you from meeting one or more goals? Could you possibly be putting on the brakes and not realize you are holding yourself back? Look around at your activity levels. Has success faded in some area of your life due to a lack of progress? Remember your mind and emotions may be allowing indecision to rule your life. And when this happens, you've already decided to fail.

Your goal right now in this exercise is to start turning off this habit if it is happening in your life. Any habit of thought that is not constructive should be disposed of. Letting go of these blocks is an important step in your journey to greater physical and mental health.

Worry leads to indecision

Fear leads to indecision

Dis-ease leads to indecision

Envy leads to indecision

Hate leads to indecision

Resentment leads to indecision

Arguments lead to indecision

How is your indecision showing up? Where are you putting on the brakes in your life?

Example:

MY WORRY IS _my company is going to have a job layoff._

My WORRYING has kept me from deciding to:

1. _purchase a new home_
2. _seriously make new friends at work_
3. _call on my boss for a raise_
4. _accept a new position that requires a relocation_
5. _pay the cost for a new degree program_

MY WORRY IS ABOUT_____

My WORRYING has kept me from deciding to:

1. _____
2. _____
3. _____
4. _____
5. _____

MY FEAR IS ABOUT _____

My FEAR has kept me from deciding to:

1. _____
2. _____
3. _____
4. _____
5. _____

MY DIS-EASE IS _____

My DIS-EASE has kept me from deciding to:

1. _____
2. _____
3. _____
4. _____
5. _____

MY ENVY IS ABOUT _____

My ENVY has kept me from deciding to:

1. _____
2. _____
3. _____
4. _____
5. _____

MY RESENTMENT HAS LED TO_____

My RESENTMENT has kept me from deciding to:

1. _____
2. _____
3. _____
4. _____
5. _____

MY HATEFUL THOUGHTS ARE ABOUT _____

My HATE has kept me from deciding to:

1. _____
2. _____
3. _____
4. _____
5. _____

MY ARGUMENTS ARE ABOUT _____

My ARGUING has kept me from deciding to:

1. _____
2. _____
3. _____
4. _____
5. _____

Indecision is a decision to fail. Where has indecision settled into your life? Keep alert to prevent this from happening in the future. Soon your journey will show you new and meaningful ways you can make all your decisions with greater ease. Keep moving so you can reach new summits of greater awareness!

Takeaways to Raise My Consciousness

A Review of Chapter Two

Success and failure can only be the results of our decisions. Each decision is made with our mind and backed by our emotions and motivation when taking any action. Once you have arrived at a decision, ideas will soon reveal themselves. Ideas arrive in the right order and sequence every time you make a decision. Learn to observe what is happening. Follow your thoughts like a detective follows all clues.

Add these enriched new ways of thinking to your day:

- You are fully capable of expressing your greatest ideas.

- Original thinking can only happen in your own mind.

- There is one Universal Mind and all of its ideas are your ideas.

- What God is doing on the grand scale of the cosmos you can do on the individual plane of experience.

- A today person experiences the fullness of life here and now.

- An immature adult lingers in the valley of questions, doubts, and fear for years.

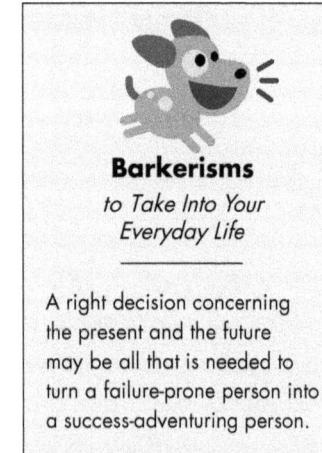

Barkerisms
to Take Into Your Everyday Life

A right decision concerning the present and the future may be all that is needed to turn a failure-prone person into a success-adventuring person.

- Stop asking, "Why did this happen to me?" Understanding the cause of a problem usually begins with a new personal insight about an old thought.

- Often, the inside of the person is the explanation for the outside of their circumstances.

- Wrong ideas bring forth incorrect decisions, often with unpleasant results.

- Most people will never know how many original ideas were hidden and covered up by their doubts.

- Ideas need you to personalize their expression in order to show up in your experience.

- The birthplace of God's intentions is found in your individual use of the One Mind.

Barkerisms
to Take Into Your Everyday Life

The way out of trouble is a way into the mind. It is not a way of facts. It is a way of ideas. Every idea you need is instantly available at the moment you need it.

"The reason most peoples' prayers are not answered is the answer or 'idea' is not in the prayer. God does not give us things, It gives us ideas. And what we do with them [ideas] produces our answer."

Rev. Dr. Lloyd George Tupper,
mentee and student of Dr. Barker

Are you looking for fresh new ideas?

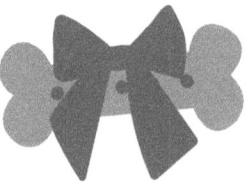

How Can My Mind Be Receptive?

Better Ideas

Dr. Barker encouraged us to discover all our right decisions wait on our personal recognition. He explained they are already in your mind.

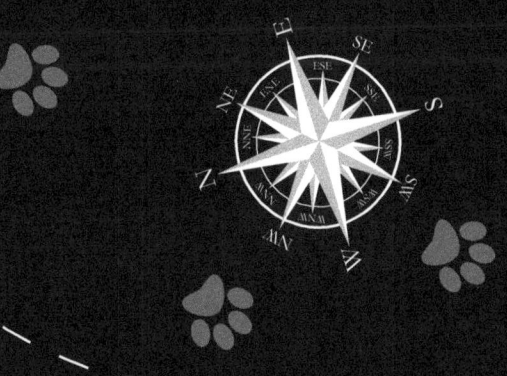

Ask Yourself: What Do I Believe?

Answer Five Questions to Start Your Journey

1

Do I believe expecting positive outcomes is a sign of a healthy mind?

2

Do I believe good ideas lead to better decisions?

3

Do I believe some of my past decisions are still placing limits on my future opportunities?

4

Do I believe I am more optimistic because I do expect some good to come into my future?

5

Do I believe what God thinks of me has weighed on my feelings of self-worth at times?

Workbook Chapter Summary

 describing the capacity of our minds to work for us, Dr. Barker reminded us that our subconscious incorporates a "mental machinery" that draws to us all the resources we need. Often, our conscious mind cannot comprehend this. Our human mind will never know all the ways and means that people, places, and things can come into our lives to fulfill our demonstrations.

It is said that the brain makes upwards of 35,000 decisions in a day. Referring to the brain as a computer does not seem outrageous. Not even Dr. Barker could have foreseen the computing power of Silicon Valley inventions and how the digital world would transform our lives in the 21st century. Yet without much technical know-how of the inner workings of such complex systems and the mobility cellular technology offers, he knew with unwavering certainty that our minds are the most powerful computing and information-gathering tool we could ever possess. How could they not be? They are all fueled by the same Universal Intelligence.

Our thoughts have no boundaries. They are not bound by time or place or even expense. Knowledge gathering is basic and fundamental to all human existence. And we can consciously choose what we want to know. Our consciousness can move into action where it knows no boundaries or limitations. Only the physical laws, while on earth, bind our physical bodies.

Dr. Barker challenges us to see ourselves as pure consciousness. He discourages us from the use of personal labels. A credit score, our grades, or a former relationship is not the truth of who we are. Don't get trapped into the good or bad of any label. Your goal is to

Barkerisms
*to Take Into Your
Everyday Life*

The unpardonable sin is that which blocks a good idea from coming into form.

know yourself on a deeper level where you can plumb the depths of new ideas and explore your intuitive nature. You are always in the process of becoming. And what you consciously choose to become becomes your reality. You can make a very long list of facts about your life, document your genealogy, analyze your family history from a swab of your DNA, or study the prescription bottles in your medicine cabinet, but none of these can ever amount to the whole truth of who you are. Yes, these are the facts of your life, but they are not the truth of who you were born to be.

Barkerisms
to Take Into Your Everyday Life

When you find out what's wrong with a person, you rarely find out what's right with him.

Honoring your intuitive nature as real and personal will help you discover correct mental thinking. Right ideas that are good and perfect for your use await your discovery. When you make a conscious decision to claim these unique ideas as your own, you have made the most strategic decision in your success plan; you have given a responsive and intelligent universe your direction. You have made an emotional attachment to some good you desire, and now you can begin to prepare yourself mentally to commit to it.

This commitment is like coupling train cars on your very own track; decision after decision will come to you with ease, allowing you to move forward. You will look back and ask, "How did I get here?" or even, "How could this happen to me?" But your inner self will whisper the truth. Can you accept and trust that God has a process of personal evolution just for you?

The emotional soil we till is the first sign of our willingness to experience our own spiritual growth. A seed of thought planted consciously by us in earnest has a very good chance of becoming real. This is when our mental machinery has been called into action. Our feelings and emotions tell us that something good is happening inside of us. Dr. Barker calls this spiritual experience "the uncontaminated you." Once you release your decision to the subconscious mind, it takes over to produce your results; it only knows to obey. You can trust this process. Your mental machinery is moving in a logical sequence to bring the resources you need for a Law of Growth to act on your choice. Remember, God is not subject to the Law of Growth, but you are. Results will take time to be made real.

Barkerisms
to Take Into Your Everyday Life
_____

All our basic problems are the results of our emotions moving through our disorganized or disorderly patterns.

A great idea is a mental equivalent of one of your heart's desires.

When Dr. Barker said, "An idea accepted is an idea demonstrated," he meant that we have accepted and claimed a better idea for ourselves. Like a gold miner of yesteryear, this claim belongs to you and you alone.

You can experience a good idea about yourself with no strain or pre-qualification. However, you must maintain your focus and not deviate from your conviction. Free your mind from all doubt. This time you are going to go on a mental diet and refrain from all worry, doubt, and fear.

Barkerisms
to Take Into Your Everyday Life
_____

An idea accepted is an idea demonstrated.

Nature always equips Its creation with everything creation needs for growth.

So decide which ideas are right for you. And once a decision is made, hold on to it tightly. Every time a new idea presents itself ask yourself if it is time to let go of an inferior thought or some lesser condition. In time, you will come to understand that past facts have no power to hold you back. If a lesser condition exists in your life, ask yourself if it's time to let it go. Remember, at all times God fills the vacuum you just created with something better, if you allow it. Indecision can only delay your good news.

Once you set yourself free to go in a new direction, something new and more rewarding will be on its way to you. Don't allow inferior thoughts to quickly slip in and fill the void; instead, fill that vacuum with some higher good you desire.

In the success process, there is only one true Universal Power, and you are using it. That power is put to good use when you decide to expand your consciousness and commit to a greater idea of yourself. You are the only one who can consciously make this choice.

Nothing is more personal or more freeing than to trust that in the Universal Mind all great ideas are individualized through you; they are waiting for your recognition and acceptance.

Each idea stands ready to ignite your imagination. The power and influence of these ideas on your whole being will be immense, if you allow it. They are the good in the world that you have been seeking. Magical Barky says it is time to accept and uncover a lasting new truth about yourself.

"Let the views of others educate and inform you, but let your decisions be a product of your own conclusions."

Jim Rohn, entrepreneur

Words, Concepts, and Phrases to Practice in Chapter Three

In a few simple words, write out what each vocabulary word means. Refer to page 10, the vocabulary section, to review and think about what you understand about each definition. The vocabulary has been written carefully and thoughtfully to help you understand spiritual terms, concepts, and practices. A new vocabulary is essential to help you deepen your understanding about what is powering your decision to bring about your desired result. Once you better understand these words and how to use them correctly, you will grow into a more evolved spiritual thinker who gets better results.

Decision Making:

_____
_____
_____
_____
_____
_____

Demonstrations:

_____
_____
_____
_____
_____
_____

Intuition:

_____
_____
_____
_____
_____
_____

Law of Growth:

_____
_____
_____
_____
_____
_____
_____
_____
_____

Law of Mind:

_____
_____
_____
_____

Subconscious Mind:

_____
_____
_____
_____
_____

Thumbs-Up Barky Says It's Time to Journal Your Impressions

Start applying what you have learned!

Writing contributes to emotional well-being, increases mental and emotional clarity, reduces stress, and increases problem-solving.

Write down your AH-HA moments, realizations, recognitions, or exclamations of sudden understanding. For example, did any of the five questions cause you to stop and ponder your answers? Did you think back on a specific life choice you made? Did the chapter summary make you think more deeply about a personal goal or decision? Are you considering how you might grow more spiritual? Perhaps one or more AH-HA moments include all of the above! *What has been stirred up inside of you? Write your impressions down here.*

_____

_____

_____

_____

_____

_____

_____

_____

_____

_____

_____

_____

_____

_____

_____

_____

_____

_____

_____

Personalized Workbook Exercises

Here Is Your Success Process

Use this simple formula:
Know what you want and by what date it shall happen.
Stop patterns of inferior thinking and begin to focus on

YOUR BEST DECISIONS EVER!

I have made my decision TO STOP WORRYING ABOUT:

I want to _____

_____

_____

I have decided what shall happen by this date: _____

I have made my decision TO STOP FEARING THE WORST ABOUT:

I want to _____

_____

_____

I have decided what shall happen by this date: _____

I have made my decision TO STOP ALL RESENTMENT ABOUT:

I want to _____

_____

_____

I have decided what shall happen by this date: _____

I have made my decision TO STOP ALL ENVY ABOUT:

I want to _____

_____

_____

I have decided what shall happen by this date: _____

I have made my decision TO STOP SOMETHING I HATE:

I want to _____

_____

_____

I have decided what shall happen by this date: _____

I have made my decision TO STOP ALL ARGUING ABOUT:

I want to _____

_____

_____

I have decided what shall happen by this date: _____

I have made my decision TO STOP BELIEVING IN DISEASE AS NORMAL:

I want to _____

_____

_____

I have decided what shall happen by this date: _____

Let's get out there and go find our best decisions ever!

EXERCISE TWO: BE SPIRITUALLY AWARE

Universal Intelligence Needs You to Rely on Spiritual Mind Treatment to Grow YOUR Spiritual Awareness!

This next exercise is going to encourage you to go deeper into the richness of your mind's ideas, ideas that are being generated from within the Universal Mind for your use alone. Here is a wonderful opportunity to do a Spiritual Mind Treatment or affirmative prayer to help you recognize your next steps. Let's use this spiritual process to help you recognize that the decisions within you need to surface to a conscious level. All solutions to your problems are also seeking your recognition.

To stimulate spiritual insights that can direct your next actions, let's state an affirmative prayer or Spiritual Mind Treatment. Here is an example you can use. Please speak the following treatment aloud or silently to yourself before you do the next exercise.

There is one Universal Creative Spirit and I know it is everywhere present. My own intelligence is responsive to this greater Universal Mind. Through this unification I am guided to make right decisions. Each arrive with purpose and clarity. My heart's desires are the focus of these decisions. Each of these ideas comes to me in right order and right time. I am grateful for all the support I require to accomplish all my good. Knowing I am clarifying my thinking for my highest and best good, I release my intention over to Universal Intelligence. I call this Intelligence God. I now accept all my good is fully expressed and in God's care. Fulfilled by the Law of Growth, which regulates the cosmos and everything on this Earth, my desires are brought into my experience in perfect order. And so it is.

Dr. Barker said that every decision requires your calm acceptance of the necessary work that follows your decision, which means the moment you make a decision get ready to take action.

Example of Your Best Ideas:

I WANT TO: (Write out your decision)

Stop worrying about turning 60 years of age and thinking I am over the hill.

Actions, steps, or ideas that come to my mind include:

1. *Consult with a specialist about products for my skin*
2. *I think it would be really fun to have a make-over*
3. *Talk with my hair stylist about a new, contemporary look*
4. *Think about dying my hair back to its original color*
5. *Assess my wardrobe; I could use more youthful clothes*

Decision #1: I CAN STOP WORRYING BECAUSE

I WANT TO (Write out your decision)

_____

_____

Actions, steps, or ideas that come to my mind include:

1. _____
2. _____
3. _____
4. _____
5. _____

Decision #2: I CAN STOP FEARING BECAUSE

I WANT TO (Write out your decision)

_____

_____

Actions, steps, or ideas that come to my mind include:

1. _____
2. _____
3. _____
4. _____
5. _____

Decision #3: I CAN STOP RESENTING BECAUSE

I WANT TO (Write out your decision)

_____

_____

Actions, steps, or ideas that come to my mind include:

1. _____
2. _____
3. _____
4. _____
5. _____

Decision #4: I CAN STOP ENVYING BECAUSE

I WANT TO (Write out your decision)

_____

_____

Actions, steps, or ideas that come to my mind include:

1. _____
2. _____
3. _____
4. _____
5. _____

Decision #5: I CAN STOP HATING BECAUSE

I WANT TO (Write out your decision)

_____

_____

Actions, steps or ideas that come to my mind include:

1. _____
2. _____
3. _____
4. _____
5. _____

Decision #6: I CAN STOP ARGUING BECAUSE

I WANT TO (Write out your decision)

_____

_____

Actions, steps, or ideas that come to my mind include:

1. _____
2. _____
3. _____
4. _____
5. _____

Decision #7: I CAN STOP ALL FOCUS ON DIS-EASE BECAUSE

I WANT TO (Write out your decision)

_____

_____

Actions, steps or ideas that come to my mind include:

1. _____
2. _____
3. _____
4. _____
5. _____

**Quizzical Barky asks, "What inferior thoughts are you willing
to replace or discard to grow more spiritually aware?"**

Takeaways to Raise My Consciousness

A Review of Chapter Three

The only primary function of your mind is to formulate a more meaningful decision to act upon. Better ideas are the essential ingredients to make all your decisions tailored to fit your goal. Your birthright is to be the best person to express those ideas and bring them to pass.

Add these new enriched ways of thinking to your day:

- On earth, no one else can determine your good better than you can.

- God has no favorites. You are It!

- Your consciousness has a purpose, not a plan set in stone.

- True intuition can only be realized and perfected by growing your self-awareness.

- Intuition is not meant to make you richer, happier, or healthier. Instead it helps you to explore more about yourself from a higher and more distinct vantage point.

- Your personal growth and evolution will unfold in orderly ways, if you let them.

Barkerisms
to Take Into Your Everyday Life

The whole world shouts about what you cannot do. It says you are a victim of the times. It measures you in terms of success and failure, heath and disease, friends and enemies. It is emphatic about your age, your life expectancy, and finances. It affirms your bank account and ultimate death. "I am consciousness" reverses all of this.

- Predicting the future is pure nonsense.

- All optimism is a belief in the future.

- Will power is useless and wastes precious energy. It is also a distraction that will take you off course.

- Optimism is your own personal expression of a spiritual potential yet to be realized.

- The depressed person is always fixated on the problem. They have created a self-imposed cycle of poverty thinking that can last a lifetime.

- Unhappy people have been spiritually declining for years.

- The creative person is always using their own unique and individual ideas to get out of a problem.

- Creative thinkers will always deeply stir the cosmos when their ideas are recognized and realized.

Barkerisms
to Take Into Your Everyday Life

There is something of God in every person. I call this Individuality. Again, I return to the premise "I am consciousness." This is a definition of you that is beyond the frame of reference known as good and evil. It is the uncontaminated you. It is you as potential.

"Everything is intelligence and the Principle of intelligence is responsiveness. Therefore the person making a decision is using their intelligence to evoke a responsiveness on the part of a greater Intelligence to have their decision fulfilled."

Rev. Dr. Lloyd George Tupper,
mentee and student of Dr. Barker

Keep moving! Your greatest ideas are ready to be discovered

How Can I Evolve Spiritually?

Happiness

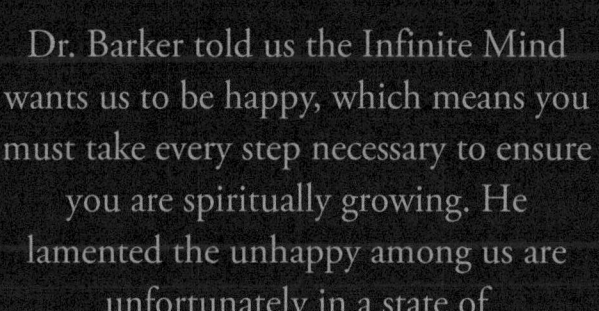

Dr. Barker told us the Infinite Mind wants us to be happy, which means you must take every step necessary to ensure you are spiritually growing. He lamented the unhappy among us are unfortunately in a state of spiritual decline.

Ask Yourself: What Do I Believe?

Answer Five Questions to Start Your Journey

1

Do I believe I have the right to be happy?

2

Do I believe I have put material things in charge of my happiness at times?

3

Do I believe unhappiness creeps in when I see the glass half-full?

4

Do I believe I have put some people in charge of my underlying sense of fulfillment?

5

Do I believe focusing on a solution is much better than focusing on the level of the problem?

Workbook Chapter Summary

hen Dr. Barker wrote about happiness, he described it as a "deep underlying sense of fulfillment." Today many products and services are produced which can make us happier and more attractive. Most people have "a gluttony of things" to help them be happier. Technology and innovation have made life simpler. Science too accelerates our rates of cure. Goods arrive faster and cheaper, delivered right to our doorsteps. All of this should make our life more enjoyable, right?

But do more apps on your phone increase your satisfaction? Can having whiter teeth make your life more deeply satisfying? The problem is that we can be so busy doing many things we fail to sort out our most important thought from all the noise. How can we do that? We turn to our conscious mind. And we can get even better results when we accept we are thinking with the Mind of God. How can any result be inferior when we are conscious of our thinking in this One Mind?

Dr. Barker declared that there is only one correct way to be happy— through a better use of our mind and better ideas. You won't find happiness through your pocketbook, your phone apps, your Facebook friends, or a superhero on your favorite channel. They are fine as things go, but ideas are your ticket to happiness. Identifying and using your better ideas stops the "Why am I unhappy?" conversation from keeping you stuck. You can no longer say "Why is my career going nowhere?" or "Why is my satisfaction so low?" when you consciously court new decisions that lead you to greater personal awareness. Letting go of lesser conditions will always be a choice. So think more, and think more, and think more about

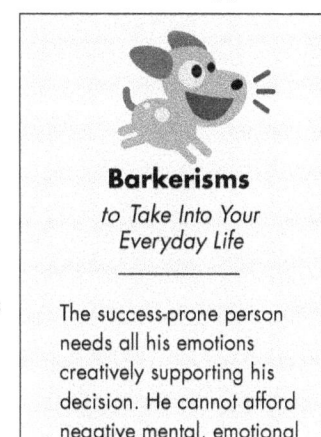

Barkerisms
to Take Into Your Everyday Life

The success-prone person needs all his emotions creatively supporting his decision. He cannot afford negative mental, emotional diversions.

Barkerisms

*to Take Into Your
Everyday Life*

Problems are to the mind
what pain is to the body.

how to use your individual awareness to raise your thoughts above your immediate conditions. The "It" in you awaits your personal recognition. Dr. Barker gave a wonderful Spiritual Mind Treatment about what God is and is doing in your life. He explained we already have every good idea we need within us. Each idea is just waiting to be revealed in our thoughts and embraced by our feelings. We should not resist these ideas or the good they bring to us. And when we accept them, we start to let go of older patterns of unhappiness or thoughts of unworthiness that have kept parts of us frozen for years. When we are ready to accept some greater good for ourselves, it's time to take action and leave the past behind. Declare these statements out loud: The one Mind, God, Infinite Good includes all that I am. It includes every idea I need to be happy and creative. I am open and receptive to the Divide Ideas in my consciousness.

Are you ready to practice God's spectacular ideas?

Dr. Barker's Treatments allow you to open up your perceptions as a spiritual practitioner of these wonderful ideas. To think correctly is to think spiritually and become more receptive to intuitive instruction; a Treatment is a positive instruction to your subconscious mind that is backed up by a good housekeeping seal of Universal Intelligence and approval by God. By practicing an affirmative prayer, you open yourself to receive your good in the present without mental reservation or hesitation. Your words represent the natural wholesomeness you seek. As you speak, your words create the spiritual prototype or mental model you imagine for

Thumbs Up Barky says Spiritual Treatment will shift your attention from a negative to a positive. Hold a positive thought long enough for it to register. Make that thought a central statement in your daily activity. Don't let anyone or anything distract you from a positive idea.

yourself. Words are so powerful when you direct them with intention. All mental efforts are worthwhile when you focus daily with conscious intention to bring about your good. You are learning the best way to give positive instruction to yourself is through the use of affirmative prayer or Spiritual Mind Treatment. Treating your own mind initiates a process to think c-o-r-r-e-c-t-l-y. Whatever you may be doing right now, wherever you may be standing, sitting, jogging, cycling, or lying down, you can do a Treatment. When spoken out loud or silently contemplated, it will help you feel an inner sense of peace and well-being. It makes God present in your immediate experience. Don't rush your thoughts. Stop and slow down the treadmill of your routine feelings and thoughts. Make your Treatment a daily practice to stop monotonous or inferior thinking from consuming every waking hour of your day. Dr. Barker called this kind of thinking "static states," and warned that they lead you to make problems for yourself with even more unsatisfactory results. He explained that Spiritual Mind Treatment is for the purpose of mental clarification that leads to purposeful insights.

Barkerisms

*to Take Into Your
Everyday Life*

Any thinking that is backed up with an emotional intent (good or bad) will get results.

Dr. Barker said unhappiness is a "misuse of your spiritually endowed creative equipment" and the only way to avoid a static, dull consciousness is to express a hunger for new ideas. He said life is a "forward-moving consciousness," and you can find happiness when you step into the rhythm of ideas flowing into your mind. Daily we can all receive intuitive instruction. Thoughts arrive in your mind every minute. And as they arrive, you choose which ones will set your course of action for that day.

The truth of greatest importance is that all your ideas come from an Infinite Mind that you are intimately connected to. You practice your individual use of this Universal Mind daily as you exercise a thought. You

Barkerisms
to Take Into Your Everyday Life

The direction of your language indicates the direction of your thinking.

have every right to exercise this Universe of Intelligence. Dr. Barker told us when we decide to be happy the whole creative action of the Universe moves instantly to act on our decision, which means being all intelligent It [God] knows what to do and how to do it.

Take this challenge to remove all inferior thoughts!

Could you write a Treatment to help you go seven days without a negative thought?

Barkerisms
to Take Into Your Everyday Life

All Life is conspiring to make you a finer and happier person.

"... What do I mean by negative thinking? Well, a negative thought is any thought of failure, disappointment, or trouble; any thought of criticism or spite or jealousy, or condemnation of others, or self-condemnation; any thought of sickness, or in short, any kind of limitation or pessimistic thinking. Any thought that is not positive or constructive in character, whether it concerns you yourself or anyone else, is a negative thought."

Emmet Fox, author of *The 7 Day Mental Diet*

Pointer Barky Says It's Time Now to Learn to Give Yourself a Treatment in Five Proven Steps

Prepared especially for the reader who desires to do a Treatment for themselves, this guide will show you how to pray affirmatively to produce better results in your life.

You'll be guided step-by-step to experience this wonderful spiritual practice. Secure a proven way to remove obstructions in your life.

TURN NOW TO PAGE 181

Words, Concepts, and Phrases
You Will Need to Practice in Chapter Four

In a few simple words, write out what each vocabulary word means. Refer to page 10, the vocabulary section, to review and think about what you understand about each definition. The vocabulary has been written carefully and thoughtfully to help you understand spiritual terms, concepts, and practices. A new vocabulary is essential to help you deepen your understanding about what is powering your decision to bring about your desired result. Once you better understand these words and how to use them correctly, you will grow into a more evolved spiritual thinker who gets better results.

Affirmative Prayer:

_____
_____
_____
_____
_____
_____

Demonstration:

_____
_____
_____
_____
_____
_____

First Cause:

_____
_____
_____
_____
_____

Law of Growth:

_____
_____
_____
_____
_____

Treatment:

_____
_____
_____
_____
_____

Additional Impressions and Notes

_____
_____
_____
_____
_____
_____
_____
_____

STEP 4

Mountaineer Barky Says It's Time to Journal Your Impressions

Reach new heights to give yourself a better view!

Writing contributes to emotional well-being, increases mental and emotional clarity, reduces stress, and increases problem-solving.

Write down your AH-HA moments, realizations, recognitions, or exclamations of sudden understanding. For example, did any of the five questions cause you to stop and ponder your answers? Did you think back on a specific life choice you made? Did the chapter summary make you think more deeply about a personal goal or decision? Are you considering how you might grow more spiritual? Perhaps one or more AH-HA moments include all of the above! *What has been stirred up inside of you? Write your impressions down here.*

_____

_____

_____

_____

_____

_____

_____

_____

_____

_____

_____

_____

_____

_____

_____

_____

Personalized Workbook Exercises

EXERCISE ONE

Making a Depth Decision to Be Happy: Which Circle of Thought Are You in?

Take a little time to study the three Decision Wheels on the following pages. Wheel One is a NO Decision. This is often where our problems begin. When Wheel One goes round and round and fosters routine thinking, we never leave behind the problems we face. Feeling static and stuck, our problematic thinking only grows.

How do you feel as you go through each Decision Wheel? What are you thinking about? How is it affecting you? Make some written or mental notes on where you find yourself today. Can you identify one or more circumstances you find yourself in with each wheel? Can you see the possibilities of moving from the NO or NOW Wheel more rapidly to get to the WOW Wheel by using what you have learned from chapter readings and exercises?

Don't make yourself wrong or bad if you don't find yourself in all cases in the WOW Wheel. It's enough to recognize where you are now. Your job is to rise above your current circumstances and recognize when you find yourself in a NO DECISION; that is when most people are stuck and confused. Your job is to recognize and identify when a NO DECISION has prevented you from an experience of greater living.

Quizzical Barky continually reminds us that a NO DECISION is actually a decision to fail. Perhaps now you have identified one or more areas of your life to consciously work on. Do you think you have some of the tools now to change the momentum and pace of moving forward in your life?

Are you here?

NO DECISION

My "No Decision" can be identified when I

- **Procrastinate**
- **Become passive**
- **Lack inspiration**

- **Feel stagnation**
- **Am wondering**
- **Am bored**

- **Am uncertain**
- **Am on the fence**

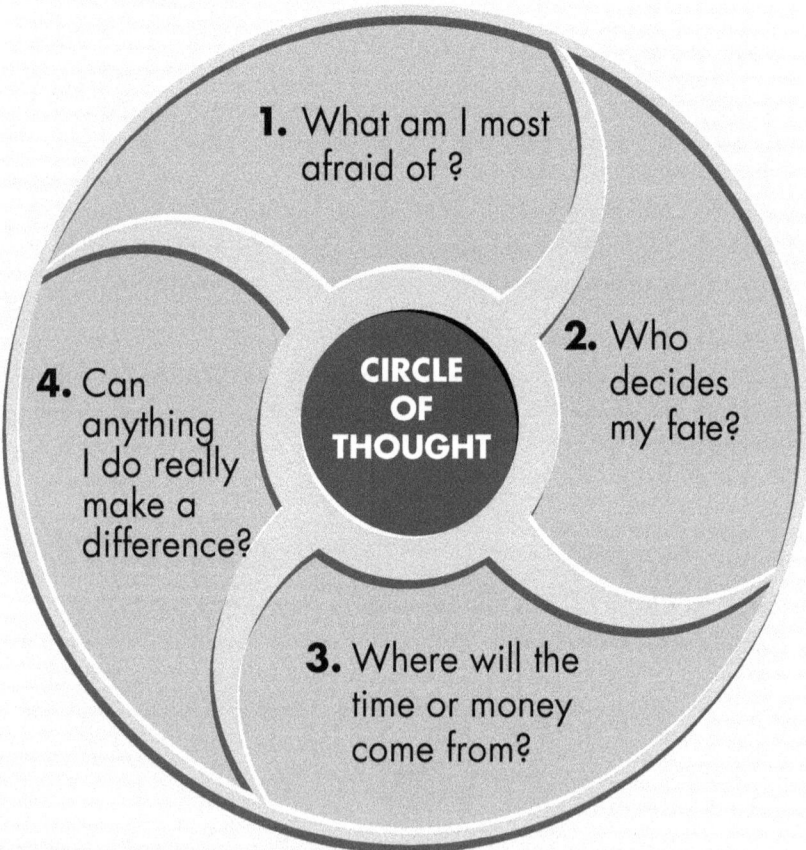

CIRCLE OF THOUGHT

1. What am I most afraid of ?

2. Who decides my fate?

3. Where will the time or money come from?

4. Can anything I do really make a difference?

Or here?

A NOW DECISION

My "Now Decision" can be identified when I

- **Feel pressured**
- **Panic**
- **Feel restlessness**

- **Am frantic**
- **Feel out of time**
- **Am in turmoil**

- **Am anxious**
- **Feel that it's now or never**

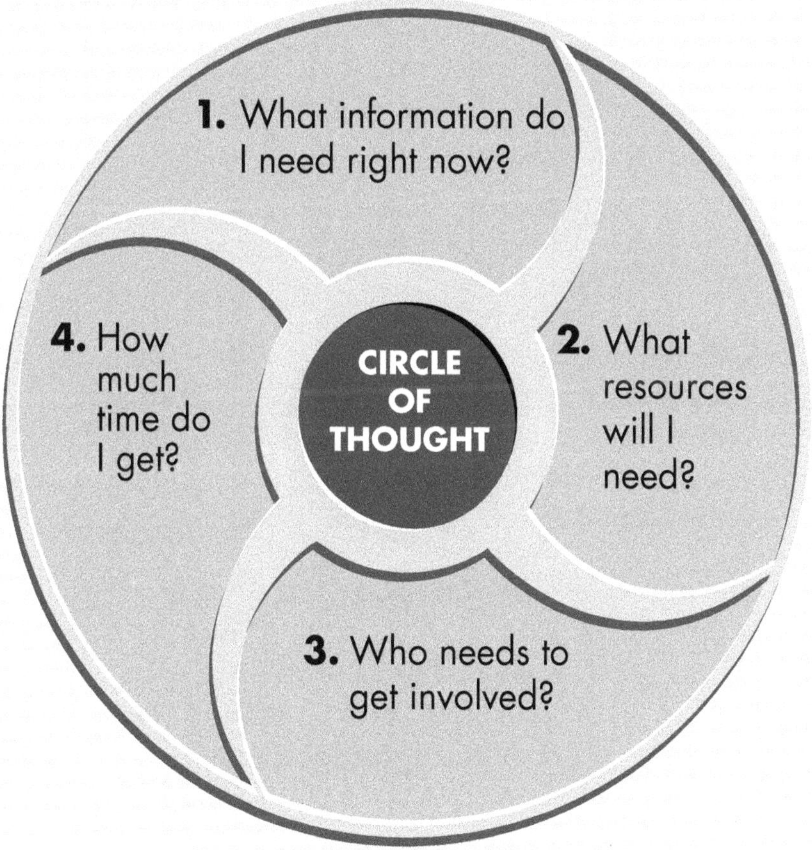

CIRCLE OF THOUGHT

1. What information do I need right now?

2. What resources will I need?

3. Who needs to get involved?

4. How much time do I get?

Or more like?

A WOW DECISION!

A "Wow Decision!" can be identified when I

- **Am hopeful**
- **Am curious**
- **Am inspired**

- **Feel totally excited**
- **Am fascinated**
- **Believe in myself**

- **Am optimistic**
- **Feel full of zest**

1. When I know which heart's desires to pursue

4. When I am confident that I can accomplish my desire

CIRCLE OF THOUGHT

2. When I connect with others who share my desire

3. When I have the courage to make the right decision

EXERCISE TWO

The Circle of Thought Wheel:
Making a Depth Decision to Be Happy

By the time you completed Chapter Three in your workbook, you had drilled down and identified your top decisions. From that moment on, you knew what you wanted to work on. You were clear! Perhaps for the first time, you made a depth decision to be happy. Dr. Barker calls these your "Normal Modes of Living." Naturally, you are going to feel some decisions are more important than others, but you gave yourself a chance to rise above your basic circumstances and see a bigger picture of your future.

After reviewing the Special Section on Treatment, you may have spent some time practicing a Treatment. This spiritual practice gives you "intuitive instruction" through your conscious connection with the Universal Mind. How did that make you feel? Can you see yourself doing a Treatment or affirmative prayer daily? If you feel you have started something new, even if it feels like baby steps, congratulations! As Barky has shown us, our job is to connect our intelligent thinking in a conscious, daily union with the Intelligence of the Universal Mind. And now you have the five proven steps of Treatment to aid you.

This important change you are feeling is really a change in your intelligent responsiveness to the Universal Mind. It is true Intelligence you are expressing! It cannot be emphasized enough that you are experiencing real Intelligence when you recognize this change in your mental knowingness. It is your individual mentality connecting to the whole of Universal Intelligence. You connect daily as well when you practice a Treatment; this allows you to pay more attention to your feelings and take charge of your thoughts. You are no longer dull, unresponsive, or stuck in a monotonous routine.

Don't be concerned if negative thoughts do come to you; that is normal and natural. Thoughts of all kinds come up to help you recognize what you need to clear out of your mentality. Remember our **A-B-C** exercise in the Special Section that helped you assess your readiness to change? You learned that you can tell yourself something different TODAY about an event that occurred just yesterday or long ago and change those negatively charged feelings into a healing. You can begin at any time to reveal your perfect self so you can move forward and express your own personal greatness.

Because it's so important, let's review that essential exercise for a moment. As we learned, the event "**A**" is neutral. However, what we tell ourselves about that event—that's the "**B**" part—can really supercharge our emotions and feelings for better or worse—that's the "**C**" part. Are you giving yourself a positive charge or a negative charge? If you feel paralyzed, dulled, and sapped of energy, you are likely stuck in an old story. It sounds and feels like Decision Wheel One, where you can get stuck in a NO decision. The old "**B**" goes round and round in your conversation, impairing your ability to move on. Could you be willing to say something different to yourself? Are you ready to have a new "**B**" conversation and release old hurts and negative emotions? If so, you are beginning to put the Circle of Thought Decision Wheel to work in your life. Now you can begin to pull yourself out of those emotional ruts and move confidently toward a WOW decision.

Remember, you are the only one in control of those private conversations. By doing your Spiritual Mind Treatment daily, you are positively charging your thoughts. Staying stuck in your old negatively charged story drains your emotional and intellectual batteries, and you are quickly exhausted. That means lots of heavy emotional baggage is carried around. Doesn't sound like much fun.

So ask yourself: are you energized by a new idea? Does each new idea encourage you to become more curious? Can you see yourself beginning to seek out new people who share your enthusiasm? And here's the big one: has certainty and confidence finally found a re-entry point back into your world?

Bravo for trying. Moving out of the rut of a NO DECISION to press onward to a NOW DECISION will give you the forward momentum to get to a WOW DECISION much faster! And isn't getting the right result becoming more important to you with every passing day?

So Quizzical Barky asks, "What is keeping you from moving toward your next goal?"

Baby Barky Believes in Tiny Steps

Dr. Barker taught that only a changed individual will have a changed experience, which means we use a spiritual and mental law in all of our demonstrations.

Barky reminds us to stay positively charged on our pathway to change. You took your first step toward personal greatness when you picked up this workbook. You have persisted and started to actualize the power of decision in your life. You may feel like you're taking baby steps at times, but you are moving toward a depth decision to be happy. The expression of new ideas—some big, some small, and some even seemingly insignificant—is so important to your progress. **Practice letting go of all lesser conditions to make room for the new!**

When you start to let go of of lesser conditions, removing them one by one, you begin to feel the acceleration of an advancing, forward-moving consciousness. You are now ready to take a NO DECISION and move it through a NOW DECISION in order to produce a WOW DECISION! If so, you are growing spiritually in your thinking.

Walk through your own Decision Wheels. Go through each question in the circle of thought and make some mental notes. Write them on the following pages as you progress through each Decision Wheel. Your ideas, regrets, concerns, and future outlook need to be expressed in order to let go of all inferior thoughts that have produced all lesser conditions in your life. This is your opportunity to become conscious of and alert to those internal wheels moving through your mental machinery on the road to success.

So if you are experiencing a....

NO DECISION, what's keeping you stuck? Is there something you are afraid of? Why are you procrastinating? Are you complacent?

_____
_____
_____
_____
_____
_____
_____
_____
_____

Do you feel the challenges that come with arriving at....

A NOW DECISION? What kind of conversation are you having with yourself? Are you feeling pressure to get something started?

_____
_____
_____
_____
_____
_____
_____
_____

If you could make your next depth decision to be happy....

To have a WOW DECISION, what change in your thinking would you need to make to move forward? Contemplate possibilities:

_____
_____
_____
_____
_____
_____
_____

"Intuition is the ability to interpret the energetic information that is always a part of every aspect of life and to use that energetic information for making wise choices—not safe, but wise. Intuition does not promise an end to all pain; in fact, pain and pleasure should not even factor into our understanding of intuition. Intuitive ability has more to do with learning to rely upon our natural wisdom than it does with developing a means of protection."

Caroline Myss, Ph.D.,
The Intuitive Healer

Additional notes and thoughts about your journey to make new Wow Decisions about happiness:

_____

_____

_____

_____

_____

_____

_____

_____

_____

_____

_____

_____

_____

_____

_____

_____

_____

_____

_____

_____

_____

_____

EXERCISE THREE:
WRITE OUT YOUR TREATMENT FOR HAPPINESS

First, use descriptive words that best describe your thoughts and ideas.

Descriptive words that help you recognize there is only one God

_____

_____

Descriptive words that unify you with this loving God

_____

_____

Description of some particular good you want and desire

_____

_____

Words of gratitude that best describe how you feel right now

_____

_____

What you want to say to release your Treatment, placing your intention into the Mind of God and Its Law of Mind

_____

_____

My Treatment for a Greater Experience of Happiness

DATE WRITTEN:_____ /_____ /_____

_____

_____

_____

_____

_____

_____

_____

_____

_____

I release my Treatment to a loving God

AND SO IT IS!

Takeaways to Raise My Consciousness

A Review of Chapter Four

Dr. Barker believed he was writing about "a very unpleasant truth" when he took the position that happiness is an inside job. In essence, we are cause to our own experiences in life, or as Dr. Barker explained, our world of effects is really the out-picturing of all our intended thoughts and associated emotions.

Dr. Barker explained that people who want to change don't make a *surface decision*, but make a *depth decision*. This is where and when he makes a key point about the traditional use of prayer. Often we use it to implore some distant deity to help us, but he said it's time to stop pretending God will extract you from all your problems. Stop all forms of separation from the all Intelligent Universal Mind that made the perfect you! It's time you learned just how powerful you are.

Dr. Barker believed that God's work was already done at your birth and that the "inside" job he spoke of was your own recognition that you have great spiritual potential. But first you must be willing to grow a spiritual consciousness to fuel that potential. Everyone is born to practice the ideas of God. Everything that happens to us comes from our own consciousness. Keep this daily in your thoughts. It's time you wake up and give yourself a Treatment to start meaningful change in your thinking!

Barkerisms
to Take Into Your Everyday Life

When you open a door for someone else, you open one for yourself.

Add these new enriched ways of thinking to your day:

- The world of your mind is the final arena to find all the joy of living.

- Frustration is an insult to God. God made you to be the greatest thinker in your life. You should never be bored again.

- Decide you have everything inside you to be happy. All your greatest ideas present a spiritual constant awaiting your recognition and agreement to use them wisely.

- Watch where your mental attention goes and you will see your emotions follow. This may be the key to changing every situation in your life.

- A meaningful change in your circumstances starts with a depth decision to be happy.

- Words have power. Use them wisely to produce what you want. And Barky says, for goodness sakes, get off that monotonous wheel of NO DECISION. Break the cycle.

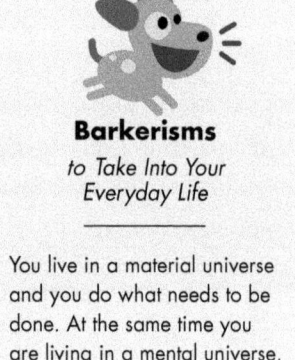

Barkerisms
to Take Into Your Everyday Life

You live in a material universe and you do what needs to be done. At the same time you are living in a mental universe, and there you rule. You are the king.

"All achievement is a marriage of idealism and great execution. The wanting alone is insufficient— there must be impeccable follow-through."

Mitch Horowitz, author

Am I Expanding My Consciousness?

Living Richly

Dr. Barker said he had proven many times in his own experience that prospering ideas are the result of a creative mental attitude focused on a prosperous way to live.

Ask Yourself:
What Do I Believe?

Answer Five Questions to Start Your Journey

1

Do I believe my current standard of living has something to do with what was in my consciousness before?

2

Do I believe with one really good decision I could dramatically change my luck?

3

Do I believe when my life feels out of balance, I am neglecting some area of my life?

4

Do I believe discarding any doubts or fears could help me prioritize what comes next in my life?

5

Do I believe some of my heart's desires just seem too impossible or too big?

Workbook Chapter Summary

DR. Barker said that only an expanded experience can come from an expanded consciousness. He places this statement at the heart and center of his belief in how to live richly. Many people, he declared, choose to use this mental and spiritual practice of an expanded forward-moving consciousness in reverse—instead of expanding their expectations, they unconsciously lessen or worse yet lower them. They think less about expecting more.

The Infinite Mind is an Infinite Mind and cannot withhold ideas from you. It knows only to give itself away by means of you. Expression is the law of life, so you are meant to fully express yourself. Infinite Mind gives itself away 24 hours a day by means of you. But if you walk around asleep all the time, it can't get through. Anything less than the fullest expression of your creativity is a misuse of your mind. Don't hold onto your No Decisions. Any notion that restricts life is false and man-made, and produces congested, clouded thinking of the worst kind. "Proclaim your wholeness to yourself," declared Dr. Barker.

> "If God makes things out of His thought before they come into manifestation, then we must use the same method. You can attract only that which you first mentally become and feel yourself to be in reality, without any doubting. A steady stream of consciousness going out into creative mind will attract a steady manifestation of conditions; a fluctuating stream of consciousness will attract the corresponding manifestation or condition in your life. We must be consistent in our attitude of mind, never wavering."
>
> Dr. Ernest Holmes, *Creative Mind and Success*, p.18
>
> Quotes from copyrighted © material owned by
> Centers for Spiritual Living d/b/a Science of Mind Publishing used with permission.

Spiritual understanding is different than the concepts within the Old and New Testament and other sacred scriptures of world religions. Dr. Barker says spiritual understanding requires acceptance and an assimilation of new vocabulary and concepts. Each individual must allow themselves to use the words God, Spirit, and Truth. Here are some IMPORTANT distinctions.

Popular understanding of the world's sacred scriptural concepts	New Thought concepts for spiritual understanding
God is a Superman.	*God is a Universal Intelligence.*
Man is born into sin and guilt.	*Man is a daily recipient of all of God's greatest qualities.*
God is separate from mortal man.	*I am God individually expressed as me.*
I am limited and born into judgment.	*I am limitless in my expression of life.*
God giveth and taketh away from me.	*God always gives itself away by means of me.*
God punishes the sins of the flesh.	*My only suffering is out of all inferior thinking about myself and the world.*
I remain guarded against mortal weaknesses.	*I live with the mental and emotional security of an expanding spiritual consciousness.*
God metes out only what I am worthy of.	*I experience the qualities of God, and I allow myself to express them daily.*
God is a spiritual mystery that I cannot comprehend.	*I operate as an individualization of the One Mind to perfectly express myself.*
My childhood God can terrify me.	*God is the Divine Givingness in all my affairs.*
A strict adherence to scripture and law commands me to be obedient.	*Infinite Mind provides an orderly system for all my ideas to express my personality.*
God is good, and all evil is the Devil's work.	*Frustrated thinking is my only sin and inferior thinking my only evil.*
The God of my understanding is a punishing God and a distant Diety.	*The impersonality of the Creative Process ensures that all my past decisions can never block my future good.*
I plead my case because God judges my whole worthiness.	*My birthright is my desire, decision, and expectancy to have the best in life.*

> Dr. Barker told us our greatest assets are our heart's desires, which means when we decide to have those experiences, we have made a depth decision to be happy. Our heart's desires are "mighty potentials" waiting only on our acceptance and recognition.
> **These should never be ignored**.

Deciding to live richly is a correct spiritual achievement of some magnitude. It can be achieved by accepting new ideas about your life. In his book *The Power of Decision*, Dr. Barker declared beauty can be seen in everything, which means you should always stand in the amazement of Spirit when you know truth and love are found in everything. All things are spiritual in nature.

Desires of your heart are not just casual hopes or daydreams. They can be realized by making a decision – a depth decision – to receive them. When you are thwarted by indecision and a belief that "I can't have it because I am not worthy," you make a decision not only to fail, but remain in a downward spiral of perpetual limitation. Stop hiding the truth from yourself; God will not withhold anything from itself or you. Only your own indecision can stand in the way of your happiness.

Barkerisms
to Take Into Your Everyday Life

We are not fighting debt. We are fighting a consciousness that produced the debt. A bill is a call to action, to produce through right thinking its equivalent.

All doubt, fear, and indecision can be discarded with correct spiritual thinking.

Dr. Barker stressed the importance of having a "prosperity consciousness." He emphasized in all endeavors to live richly it is vital to understand that money is God in action. To this end, the most intelligent response to money comes by exercising an open and total awareness of what God is doing in your life. Think of it as your "prosperity consciousness" moving through God's bank account of ideas.

Barkerisms
to Take Into Your Everyday Life

Consistent expectation of good is a sign of an adult, healthy, mature mind.

Dr. Robert Bitzer, a minister and colleague of Dr. Barker, believed wealth

Barkerisms
to Take Into Your Everyday Life

A failure is not necessarily the person who is bankrupt. A failure is anyone who, either through his own ignorance or his acceptance of situations apparently beyond his control, has resigned himself to some form of expression which is frustrating rather than creative. This causes an emotional conflict in his subconscious mind, producing lack of ease, a sense of guilt, and a feeling of insecurity.

was one of the four basic elements of life, along with health, happiness, and love. He said, "For life to be fully expressed, these four elements must be in perfect and complete balance." Dr. Bitzer explained that if one area in life was out of order, if you were poor in your circumstances regarding money or health, for example, that you were neglecting that area of your life. If you bring into your life a belief that you shouldn't have money, all your financial demonstrations will prove you right. Whatever you bring into your consciousness, you are going to live with.

Words, Concepts, and Phrases
to Practice in Chapter Five

In a few simple words, write out what each vocabulary word means. Refer to page 10, the vocabulary section, to review and think about what you understand about each definition. The vocabulary has been written carefully and thoughtfully to help you understand spiritual terms, concepts, and practices. A new vocabulary is essential to help you deepen your understanding about what is powering your decision to bring about your desired result. Once you better understand these words and how to use them correctly, you will grow into a more evolved spiritual thinker who gets better results.

Consciousness:

_____
_____
_____
_____
_____
_____

Law of Mind:

_____
_____
_____
_____
_____
_____

New Thought:

_____

_____

_____

_____

_____

_____

Additional Impressions and Notes

_____

_____

_____

_____

_____

_____

_____

_____

_____

_____

_____

_____

_____

_____

_____

_____

_____

_____

STEP 4

Pointer Barky Says It's Time to Journal Your Impressions

Seriously good ideas turn into prosperous outcomes!

Writing contributes to emotional well-being, increases mental and emotional clarity, reduces stress, and increases problem-solving.

Write down your AH-HA moments, realizations, recognitions, or exclamations of sudden understanding. For example, did any of the five questions cause you to stop and ponder your answers? Did you think back on a specific life choice you made? Did the chapter summary make you think more deeply about a personal goal or decision? Are you considering how you might grow more spiritual? Perhaps one or more AH-HA moments include all of the above! *What has been stirred up inside of you? Write your impressions down here.*

_____

_____

_____

_____

_____

_____

_____

_____

_____

_____

_____

_____

_____

_____

_____

_____

_____

_____

Personalized Workbook Exercises

EXERCISE ONE

Competitive & Comparison Thinking

— VERSUS —

Original Thinking

"Only original thinking is productive in your experience; not competitive thinking, not comparison thinking, but original thinking." (*Barkerisms*, p. 73)

Let's see how far you have come to living a richer, more fulfilling life. Using the three Decision Wheels from Chapter 4, let's see if we can uncover hidden influences that can cloud and limit your original thoughts and ideas in all aspects of your life. Once you consciously recognize how these inferior thoughts produce lesser conditions in your career, your family life, your relationships, and overall motivation to advance your professional and personal life, you can begin to discard them.

Your goal in Chapter Five is to avoid comparison and competitive thinking altogether. Also, raise your awareness of how others may respond to you when you express original ideas or thoughts of your own. Watch for possible negative reactions and quick judgments so you can recognize how these expectations can STOP the Decision Wheel from moving forward. In any area of your life, allowing comparison thinking immediately puts the brakes on your motivation, especially when you desire to pursue your own original ideas and goals at work or at home. Stop any cycle of inferior thoughts that are leading you to a decision to fail.

Comparison thinking always limits me and leads me to a "NO" decision

"I am just not good enough."	*Causes blockages and low self-esteem.*
"My fate is sealed."	*Leaves you uninspired.*
"I just don't know where to begin."	*Makes you question your intellect.*
"It must be perfect."	*Promotes procrastination every time.*
"That's just the way it is."	*Makes us unable to try something different.*
"If only I had been given a chance."	*Adds to our feelings of unworthiness.*

Competitive thinking
can instantly launch a "NOW" decision

"You have one chance to get this right."   *You question if you are smart enough.*

"There's no use in trying to get ahead."   *You feel pressured to act quickly.*

"If I had only started years earlier."   *You feel left behind or behind the 8 ball.*

"The clock is ticking."   *You feel you have already lost ground.*

"Why didn't I think of that!"   *You begin thinking if only you knew how.*

"This is once in a lifetime."   *You ponder if all your chances are used up.*

Original thinking
leads me to a "WOW" decision!

"I have a hunch that...."   *You see that you have options and choices.*

"It doesn't get better than this."   *Life starts feeling better than you imagined.*

"That's something I can believe in!"

"What a surprise to learn I could..."   *Optimism and curiosity about the future abound.*

"Who would have ever thought?"   *The unexpected allows spontaneity.*

Your heart's desires become a reality.

Magical Barky asks, "Are you using original thinking today?"

EXERCISE TWO

First, read Dr. Barker's opinion below about open-mindedness and flexibility. Now reflect back on comparative or competitive thinking in the last exercise. What is it costing you in love, health, or wealth to hold on to your limited thinking? Below, briefly revisit any of your current life concerns and write them down. Now ask yourself if your goals and desires are getting caught up in comparative or competitive thinking. Can you imagine yourself moving from a NOW Decision to a WOW Decision if you eliminate those obstructions? You will move more quickly to your desired WOW Decision when you let go of your hurts, expectations of others, and competitive thinking.

Dr. Barker explained we must pay an inner cost to have an open mind. We must give up our hurts, errors, negative assertions and self-righteousness to experience a fuller self-expression of our wealth, health, love and creativity. By letting go of these inferior thoughts and emotions we create an open channel for greater ideas and whole thinking.

CURRENT GOALS AND DESIRES	COMPARATIVE OR COMPETITIVE THINKING
#1	What are your feelings and thoughts?
_____	_____
_____	_____
_____	_____
_____	_____
#2	
_____	_____
_____	_____
_____	_____
#3	
_____	_____
_____	_____
_____	_____

CURRENT GOALS AND DESIRES

#4

_____
_____
_____
_____

#5

_____
_____
_____
_____

#6

_____
_____
_____
_____

#7

_____
_____
_____
_____

COMPARATIVE OR COMPETITIVE THINKING

What are your feelings and thoughts?

_____
_____
_____
_____

_____
_____
_____
_____

_____
_____
_____
_____

_____
_____
_____
_____

EXERCISE THREE

Let's see what you could say to yourself today that could turn comparative or competitive thinking into a WOW Decision.

For example, one concern may be about retirement and your ability to travel. This can limit your joy and outlook about getting out and going to new destinations. You have decided you cannot control what other people choose to do in their retirement and have decided to work on your own plans. Now how would you turn that into a WOW Decision? Here are some things you can say to yourself! "What if I stopped expecting my spouse to plan a 2nd honeymoon? Where have I always talked about going?" or "Imagine if we bought that little cottage by the sea. What's stopping us?"

CURRENT GOALS AND DESIRES	WOW THINKING
	What could you say to uplift yourself?
#1	What can others say to support you?
#2	
#3	

CURRENT GOALS AND DESIRES

WOW THINKING

What could you say to uplift yourself?
What can others say to support you?

#4

_____   _____
_____   _____
_____   _____
_____   _____

#5

_____   _____
_____   _____
_____   _____
_____   _____

#6

_____   _____
_____   _____
_____   _____
_____   _____

#7

_____   _____
_____   _____
_____   _____
_____   _____

EXERCISE FOUR:
WRITE OUT YOUR TREATMENT FOR RICHER LIVING

First, write out some words that best describe your thoughts and ideas.

Descriptive words that help you recognize there is only one God

_____

_____

Descriptive words that unify you with this loving God

_____

_____

Your description of some particular good you want and desire

_____

_____

Your words of gratitude that best describe how you feel right now

_____

_____

What you want to say to release your Treatment, placing your intention into the Mind of God and Its Law of Mind

_____

_____

My Treatment for a Greater Experience of Richer Living

DATE WRITTEN: ____ / ____ / ____

_____

_____

_____

_____

_____

_____

_____

_____

_____

I release my Treatment to a loving God

AND SO IT IS!

Takeaways to Raise My Consciousness

A Review of Chapter Five

The Danger of Complacency lesson by Dr. Barker from the previous chapter is worth repeating. Your personal success strategy is about having a richer and fuller life when your decisions and the decision to act support it.

The Dangers of Complacency

Complacency is an evil. It has no place in the creative process. When it enthralls your mind, subconscious trouble begins. It may be months or years before you are aware of the disintegration it has produced. You may laugh it off, but the degenerative process continues until you wake up. Eventually, some serious problem arises which stops you short and makes you re-evaluate your consciousness. Suddenly you realize that you have been drifting and not creating. You have relaxed in the false comfort of routines and paid no heed to new ideas. Your thinking and conversations are out-of-date, even though respectable. You are caught in the dying mechanism of mind. The mechanism is working this way because you have unconsciously given up living.

(*The Power of Decision*, p. 75)

Add these new enriched ways of thinking to your day:

- It is abnormal and unnecessary to live half-heartedly.

- Your situation reacts in accordance to your mind and not someone else's.

- An expanded consciousness will expand your experience.

- As a receiver of an infinite number of ideas, you are given the total Intelligence of the Universe to use.

- God as Mind can lead you to all kinds of new thoughts if you allow it.

Barkerisms
to Take Into Your Everyday Life

When you operate your consciousness as a receiving station for the imprints of the world, you have relegated the Divine Authority of your being to a place outside yourself, and you become a puppet on a string.

Barkerisms
to Take Into Your Everyday Life

We must live purposefully from within instead of accidentally from without.

- You are the right person in the right place, doing the right work to achieve the highest creative expression for your growth.

- A person who lives the full life has nothing to fear. Every today is tomorrow amplified.

- Every tomorrow is simply a rearrangement of today.

- Most desires can be thwarted by indecision. All heart's desires must be pursued and NEVER pushed away.

- Money cannot solve your problems. The solution to your problem is in the ideas your mind is given by Universal Intelligence. Learn to recognize you are the ideal person to solve those problems.

- Money problems are created by your mind, not your checkbook.

- A prosperity consciousness is a thought enhanced and speeded up by a sincere desire to live in integrity with spiritual principles.

- Always place the emphasis of your thoughts on the goal of having a balanced life.

- Use those thoughts to emphasize how you will demonstrate your creative expression.

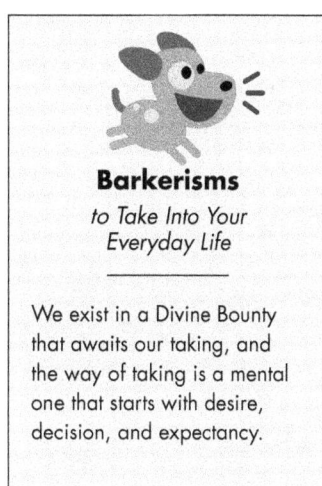

Barkerisms
to Take Into Your Everyday Life

We exist in a Divine Bounty that awaits our taking, and the way of taking is a mental one that starts with desire, decision, and expectancy.

- Don't confuse the money you make with how you are expressing your gifts and talents. Having a money consciousness is in an entirely separate category of expression.

Barkerisms
to Take Into Your Everyday Life

Our expectations are like a mental barometer. They indicate your subconscious thought patterns. They will indicate where changes need to be made.

"Our wealth can be determined only from the standpoint of our ability to use, appropriate, to express. That is the only measure we have of wealth."

Dr. Robert Bitzer, minister

Can My Thoughts Change My Body?

Physical and Mental Health

Dr. Barker said there is a "spiritual wealth of healing power within you." This explains why the Infinite Mind knows nothing about illness in matters of your health. He said your recovery from illness is certain when you start thinking as It [God] is thinking. God always stands ready to give you a more perfect self-expression of health and energy when you allow it.

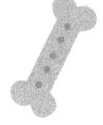

Ask Yourself:
What Do I Believe?

Answer Five Questions to
Start Your Journey

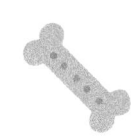

Do I believe what I have accepted about aging could be affecting my health?

Do I believe a negatively-held belief can impact my overall well-being?

Do I believe sickness has a particular psychology all its own?

Do I believe taking care of my body may not be enough if I do not have healthy attitudes?

Do I believe my mind plays a role in how my body heals after an injury or hospitalization?

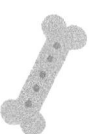

Workbook Chapter Summary

Barker said, "Health is a **yes** system and disease is a **no** system," which explains why our conscious thoughts and subconscious mind have such a compelling influence on building a healthy body. Dr. Barker said healing through spiritual means requires in the individual a desire and a willingness to change a basic subconscious pattern of belief in order to work effectively. Dr. Ernest Holmes, who is credited with perfecting the steps of a scientific form of affirmative prayer in his classic work *The Science of Mind*, saw health as perfection within the individual. He believed in spiritual mind Treatment to heal a condition was an endeavor "to arrive at a conclusion of perfection" and an opportunity to turn faith into "a dynamic use of spiritual Power" for healing purposes.

Dr. Barker felt life should be viewed as a spiritual experience and as such we can practice Spiritual Mind healing routinely in all our affairs. If the public took the time to study the foundation of the science of prayer—which is the purpose of this workbook—everyone could benefit from a personalized basic practice of Treatment in their own lives. Dr. Barker said, "The subconscious mind" is the operating system of the body, which explains why a person cannot create a healthy body until the conscious mind has made a decision to act in matters of health. He stressed the conscious mind must act authoritatively on a decision first before the subconscious mind can start to create a healthy body. This is a **WOW Decision** of some magnitude and is why Doctors Barker and Holmes advocated for an affirmative form of Treatment to intentionally set in motion a **"yes"** system for all health and wellness matters.

> **Barkerisms**
> *to Take Into Your Everyday Life*
>
> We cannot grow by associating only with the people who like what we like. The purpose of any close relationship is not for similarity of thought but for difference.

In matters of health, drug use or surgery alone are how we are often socialized to think of cures in Western cultures. We are taught and encouraged to respond to every health issue through these two methods

Dr. Barker always reminded us to select our ideas as carefully as we select our food.

alone. Dr. Barker called this way of thinking "medical conditioning," and said that academic science alone explains everything to our society, leaving society to consider no other options. Our families are taught to subscribe to this approach in our care of others. Our media outlets and advertising - whether print, TV, cable, outdoor marketing, or digital media - promote and endorse this Western system of health. Our pharmaceutical companies and their incentive programs and marketing make us believe we cannot live without drugs or be happy and healthy unless we use their products and procedures.

Barkerisms
to Take Into Your Everyday Life

The healing of sickness must embody spiritual growth or the sickness will return.

Having a relationship with God is our source for prevention and fostering good physical and mental health. This takes time and mental discipline to practice and understand, a primary benefit of this self-study that adds a complimentary addition to all your pathways to better health. Most people find the expediency of the checkbook a quick fix to everything, especially when a health issue arises. This is often the first measure of certainty people seek. "… as to God," states Dr. Barker, "they are indefinite."

Modern medicine, he believed, had earned the right to be respected due to so many advances in research, medicine, and pharmacology over the previous 100 years. After all, Dr. Barker understood these solutions too were examples of the knowledge and wisdom of God's greater ideas applied to practical problems of society at large.

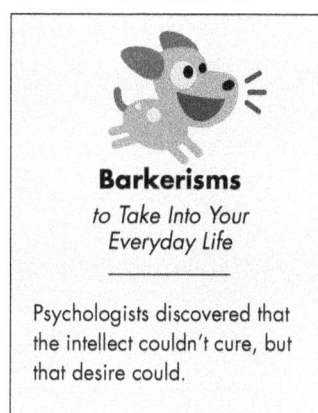

Barkerisms
to Take Into Your Everyday Life

Psychologists discovered that the intellect couldn't cure, but that desire could.

But should we wait for the achievement of others to solve our problems or find better solutions? Dr. Barker believed Treatment was the most constructive and practical form of affirmative prayer that can be done by anyone. He believed that praising our bodies and good health had as much impact on our overall well-being as praise and recognition had on our professional accomplishments. Dr. Barker stressed the "normalcy and value of health" as a basis for organizing your thoughts, which means the more you impress your "**yes**" thoughts of better health upon your subconscious mind the more secure you will be in all matters of health.

Dr. Barker said that when it comes to physical healing, the first step is to look at what is in your consciousness.

How many health issues could have been avoided altogether if a spiritual foundation of ideas and beliefs had been applied regularly to support your physical and mental health?

His colleague and fellow New Thought leader Dr. Holmes put it another way, believing all demonstrations in life began as imagined outcomes, and from these visual images our ideas about them would naturally follow. Supported by our beliefs [once we are certain of them] these images and ideas form an inner, spiritual prototype or model of our thoughts, good or bad. Once this model of thought is accepted by us, our subconscious mind goes into action. It is here our demonstration(s) are carried out by the Law of Growth. Dr. Holmes said, if a physical healing is to occur in our lives, "one must rise above the belief, the ideas, and the form which produced the disease."

"I used to believe that we must choose between science and reason on one hand, and spirituality on the other, in how we lead our lives. Now I consider this a false choice. We can recover the sense of sacredness, not just in science, but in perhaps every area of life."

Larry Dossey, M.D., author of
Reinventing Medicine

Words, Concepts, and Phrases to Practice in Chapter Six

In a few simple words, write out what each vocabulary word means. Refer to page 10, the vocabulary section, to review and think about what you understand about each definition. The vocabulary has been written carefully and thoughtfully to help you understand spiritual terms, concepts, and practices. A new vocabulary is essential to help you deepen your understanding about what is powering your decision to bring about your desired result. Once you better understand these words and how to use them correctly, you will grow into a more evolved spiritual thinker who gets better results.

Affirmative Prayer:

_____
_____
_____
_____
_____
_____

Demonstrations:

_____
_____
_____
_____
_____
_____

First Cause:

_____
_____
_____
_____
_____
_____

Spiritual Evolution:

_____
_____
_____
_____
_____
_____

Additional Impressions and Notes

_____
_____
_____
_____
_____
_____
_____
_____
_____
_____
_____
_____
_____

STEP 4

Magical Barky Says It's Time to Journal Your Impressions

Becoming your best self is a powerful achievement!

Writing contributes to emotional well-being, increases mental and emotional clarity, reduces stress, and increases problem-solving.

Write down your AH-HA moments, realizations, recognitions, or exclamations of sudden understanding. For example, did any of the five questions cause you to stop and ponder your answers? Did you think back on a specific life choice you made? Did the chapter summary make you think more deeply about a personal goal or decision? Are you considering how you might grow more spiritual? Perhaps one or more AH-HA moments include all of the above! **What has been stirred up inside of you? Write your impressions down here.**

_____

_____

_____

_____

_____

_____

_____

_____

_____

_____

_____

_____

_____

_____

_____

_____

_____

_____

Personalized Workbook Exercises

EXERCISE ONE

"Is there something you want to do that seems impossible? Then make a study of all the reasons why you *can* do it instead of all the reasons you cannot— and you will do it." (*Barkerisms*, p. 20)

Let's examine some notions and popularized beliefs about health to see if you agree more with beliefs held by the public or by Dr. Barker. Look at both sides of the conversation about health and well-being and decide where you find your allegiance growing.

The public's generally held beliefs about health	Dr. Barker's strongly held beliefs about health and well-being
You are what you eat!	I am what I think! My body always responds to my beliefs about it.
I say, "I am sick to death about ...."	My subconscious thinking always wins out.
With medicine there is certainty. Academic science explains everything. Sickness is just part of growing older.	As to God, I am definite about my faith. Money cannot solve all my problems. The normalcy of health can be impressed upon my subconscious, and at any age.
Dieting and a membership to a gym are important to getting healthy.	Maintaining sound health is a mental discipline I must practice daily.
It is important to take good care of your body.	Healthy attitudes of mind (and body) guarantee I will be healthy.
Our society gives great attention to sickness.	Sickness has a particular psychology of its own. It not only conditions my body; it also conditions my mind if I let it.
Your body is your health.	As a person seeking health, I have decided to be well. My health is not my body alone but a state of consciousness that permeates my whole body. I can do my Treatment as a daily spiritual practice for my health.
You will die from old age or from an Illness; one or the other will get you.	Over weeks, months, or years my subconscious can gradually build a sick body if I let it. But I choose not to.

EXERCISE TWO

Think about your views on health over the years. Score yourself below and see if your workbook and readings have helped you gain a new perspective. Would you use Treatment or affirmative prayer in a health crisis now? Have you gained new ways of thinking about why disease occurs? Is there a lack of ease in your thoughts about your health? Can you see a connection between a thought pattern you have uncovered and a physical ailment you may be experiencing? **What's in your Mind?**

New Thoughts, Beliefs, and Attitudes About Health

My Own Health and Well-Being: What Do I Believe?

	Not sure I believe	Yes, convincing information	I can believe and start practicing
My body reflects what I consciously think about health and aging.	1	5	10
My subconscious thoughts produce my overall health and well-being.	1	5	10
Sickness does not have to be part of growing older.	1	5	10
I cannot neglect healthy attitudes of mind if I want to be healthy over my lifetime.	1	5	10
Sickness has a particular psychology of its own. It not only conditions my body; it also conditions my mind.	1	5	10
My health is not my only my body but a state of consciousness that permeates it. I no longer accept sickness as normal.	1	5	10
I believe that over a period of weeks, months, or even years my subconscious can gradually build a sick body.	1	5	10
My body is responsive to new beliefs and healthier attitudes about myself.	1	5	10
My mental health can improve with orderly and new ways of thinking about myself.	1	5	10
My quality of life improves when my consciousness is free of negative thoughts and feelings.	1	5	10

EXERCISE THREE:
WRITE OUT YOUR TREATMENT FOR GREATER HEALTH

First, write out some descriptive words that best describe your thoughts and ideas.

Descriptive words that help you recognize there is only one God:

_____

_____

Descriptive words that unify you with this loving God:

_____

_____

Your description of some particular good you want and desire:

_____

_____

Your words of gratitude that best describe how you feel right now:

_____

_____

What you want to say to release your Treatment, placing your intention into the Mind of God and Its Law of Mind:

_____

_____

My Treatment for Greater Health in My Experiences
DATE WRITTEN: ____ / ____ / ____

_____

_____

_____

_____

_____

_____

_____

_____

_____

I release my Treatment to a loving God

AND SO IT IS!

Takeaways to Raise My Consciousness

A Review of Chapter Six

Add these new enriched ways of thinking to your day:

- People must decide to be well.

- Beliefs about your body influence your health.

- The subconscious always wins out in the matter of health.

- When you emphasize to your mind that God is life, health, strength and vitality will follow more easily.

- Illness is not normal.

- The Infinite Mind only knows Itself as health. Your recovery is certain when you believe you are thinking with the Intelligence of this Infinite Mind.

- Health is a real mental discipline. An occasional emphasis on health or diet and personal habits is completely ineffective.

Barkerisms
to Take Into Your Everyday Life

It is psychologically damaging to be afraid of the future.

- Health is necessary to keep your individual consciousness at a high level of functioning. There is no room for mental congestion.

- Health is a state of consciousness that permeates your body.

- Your consciousness was created to be a healthy mechanism for operating at your best in this world.

- You cannot maintain consistent good health without the mental and emotional discipline to have a healthy mind.

Barkerisms
to Take Into Your Everyday Life

What you praise prospers.
What you condemn withers.

Are your decisions leading you to a fuller and more balanced quality of life?

Will your next steps put you on a spiritual pathway to personal and professional growth?

What Could Help Me Awaken My Mind?

Creativity

Dr. Barker told us that spiritual thinking is the key to experiencing all of your greatest ideas. He declared this form of "awakened thinking" becomes the highest and best use of your conscious mind and can only result in a more enlightened, spiritual path to personal and professional growth.

Ask Yourself:
What Do I Believe?

Answer Five Questions to
Start Your Journey

1

Do I believe creative thinking is a great way to
awaken more of my senses?

2

Do I believe inspiration is more a function of the
Spirit within me and less about my intellect?

3

Do I believe what limits me in life can also place
limitations on my imagination?

4

Do I believe I can improve my circumstances by
becoming a more creative person?

5

Do I believe there is no quicker way to make
myself ill, miserable, or poverty-minded than to
have a closed mind?

Workbook Chapter Summary

DR. Barker gave utmost importance to why ideas paved the way to a happier and more creative life. He spoke about it throughout his career. In essence, you were born to express ideas uniquely suited for your use and distribution. Coming to understand how to become a conduit for those ideas and fulfill their perfect expression with each new demonstration is your goal throughout life.

The only thing that could obstruct the creative flow of ideas are established, negative thoughts and emotions you entertain daily. The truth about you is that you were born to receive and generate unique ideas and use them for your own personal greatness. Anything that places limits on your creative expression equates to a form of mental/physical congestion. Dr. Barker called this an "untruth" and a "sin at the level of mind."

> *Gone are the negative beseechings to a distant power. Today great masses of people are aware that the nature of life as you live it, here and now, has within itself the creative power of accomplishment. But only those who dare to emerge from the accepted beliefs of the crowd can prove this.* (Barker, *Treat Yourself to Life*, p.4)

He believed creative thinking was achieved through awakened thinking and that spiritual thinking formed the foundation of both. According to Dr. Barker, using your mind to receive and explore ideas that are right for you is the most positive form of mental action you can have in life. By using your God-given faculty of conscious choice over these ideas, you are replicating the same Divine Creative Process used by the Mind of God. Dr. Barker says this is "the highest use of mind by man," which explains why he was so passionate in his lifetime to instill his message upon a new generation. And now your turn has come to be part of the next!

Words, Concepts, and Phrases to Practice in Chapter Seven

In a few simple words, write out what each vocabulary word means. Refer to page 10, the vocabulary section, to review and think about what you understand about each definition. The vocabulary has been written carefully and thoughtfully to help you understand spiritual terms, concepts, and practices. A new vocabulary is essential to help you deepen your understanding about what is powering your decision to bring about your desired result. Once you better understand these words and how to use them correctly, you will grow into a more evolved spiritual thinker who gets better results.

Barkerisms
to Take Into Your Everyday Life

The universal Principle of Life is that of a creative Mind, a creative Intelligence, which acts through your mind producing around you what is *in* your mind.

Awakened Thinkers:

_____
_____
_____
_____
_____
_____
_____
_____

Intelligence:

_____
_____
_____
_____
_____
_____
_____

Intuition:

_____

_____

_____

_____

_____

_____

Modern Definition of God:

_____

_____

_____

_____

_____

_____

Barkerisms
*to Take Into Your
Everyday Life*

A creative person is a person
who is releasing original ideas
in a successful pattern.

Universal Intelligence:

_____

_____

_____

_____

_____

_____

Barkerisms
*to Take Into Your
Everyday Life*

Start clearing the now in order
to have what you want in the
future.

Universal Mind:

_____
_____
_____
_____
_____
_____
_____

Additional Impressions and Notes

_____
_____
_____
_____
_____
_____
_____
_____
_____
_____
_____
_____
_____

Happy Barky Says It's Time to Journal Your Impressions

Creative ideas are always something to smile about!

Writing contributes to emotional well-being, increases mental and emotional clarity, reduces stress, and increases problem-solving.

Write down your AH-HA moments, realizations, recognitions, or exclamations of sudden understanding. For example, did any of the five questions cause you to stop and ponder your answers? Did you think back on a specific life choice you made? Did the chapter summary make you think more deeply about a personal goal or decision? Are you considering how you might grow more spiritual? Perhaps one or more AH-HA moments include all of the above! *What has been stirred up inside of you? Write your impressions down here.*

_____

_____

_____

_____

_____

_____

_____

_____

_____

_____

_____

_____

_____

_____

_____

_____

_____

_____

_____

Personalized Workbook Exercises

EXERCISE ONE

Let's assess your readiness to be that navigable channel for creative ideas. Remember in Chapter Five when you reviewed competitive and comparative thinking vs. original thinking? Recall how you went from a NO Decision to a NOW Decision and saw yourself moving to a WOW Decision. Assess where you are now in your experiences of having new and creative ideas. Are you awakening to your greater self?

Qualities of a
CLOSED MIND

Dr. Barker said the quickest way to make yourself ill, miserable, and poverty minded is to have a closed mind.

A built-up mental fortress

Being mentally/physically congested

Unconsciously rejecting life

Suspicious of new ideas

Stuck in old ruts of thinking

Only half-living; a daydreamer

Resigned to situations you believe are impossible to escape

Having obsolete thinking that seeks to recreate the past in the present

Having withering spiritual muscles

Getting bogged down in the quandaries of doubt, fear, and negative speculation

Mental calcification

Qualities of an
OPEN MIND

Dr. Barker said the open-minded person is invincible when a decision comes with expectancy, curiosity, and inspiration.

Awakened thinking

Taking initiative is mental action

Being present with your true self

Enjoy being an explorer of your inner self

Willingness to fast from all negatives

Having a God that is up-to-date and active

Using a law of mental expansion daily

Willingness to grasp at an infinite number of ideas in the present and the future

All things are possible to "they who daily stir up the gift of God within"

Allowing curiosity to be the primary creative driver of thoughts in your mind

Unafraid of spiritual ideas that move you off dead center

Which mind in you is winning out?

EXERCISE TWO

Reflect on the following qualities of an open mind. Dr. Barker explained your health, wealth, love, and full self-expression come at a cost. He said in your willingness to become more flexible and open-minded, you must release those thoughts you have been carrying around in error – "your hurts and negative assertions," which he cautioned can keep your mind resistant and impervious to better ideas. So can you say you are flexible now and willing to practice spiritual thinking daily?

Do You Have the Qualities of an Open Mind?

"Are you active, up-to-date, and living in the present?"

Are You Flexible?

"With expectancy, curiosity, inspiration, and decision, the open-minded man [person] is invincible."

	Not sure I believe	Yes, convincing information	I can believe and start practicing
Experiencing awakened thinking now	1	5	10
Believing mental action is self-fulfilling	1	5	10
Praying to a God who is always present	1	5	10
Becoming an explorer of my heart's desires	1	5	10
Willing to fast from all negatives	1	5	10
Having a God that is up-to-date and present in my experiences now	1	5	10
Accepting that I live under a law of mental expansion	1	5	10
Willing to accept new ideas that remove congested thinking	1	5	10
Believing all good things are possible	1	5	10
Using curiosity as the primary creative action that moves my mind toward my goals	1	5	10
Being unafraid of spiritual reflection	1	5	10

EXERCISE THREE:
WRITE OUT YOUR TREATMENT FOR CREATIVITY

First, write out descriptive words that describe your thoughts and ideas.

Descriptive words that help you recognize a God that is present:

_____

_____

Descriptive words that unify you with this loving, present God:

_____

_____

Description of some particular good you want and desire NOW:

_____

_____

Words of gratitude that describe how you feel right now:

_____

_____

What you want to say to release your Treatment, placing your intention into the Mind of God and Its Law of Mind:

_____

_____

My Treatment to Bring Creative Ideas Into My Experience

DATE WRITTEN: _____ / _____ / _____

_____

_____

_____

_____

_____

_____

_____

_____

_____

I release my Treatment to a loving God

AND SO IT IS!

Takeaways to Raise Your Consciousness

A Review of Chapter Seven

Add these new enriched ways of thinking to your day:

- Many people are not interested in being inspired. "What is the use?" they may ask. This is an unnatural decision to live half-heartedly.

- A dull person has unconsciously rejected life.

Barkerisms
to Take Into Your Everyday Life

You will always get the average until you select the best.

- A law of mental expansion uses the creative process of the Law of Growth to bring about a balanced life over a lifetime.

- Your mental conditioning [way of thinking] will either lead to you becoming an average person or a person achieving great personal success.

- By directing your thought you have the totality of consciousness [Universal Intelligence] on your side. Grasp infinite ideas and you you will have access to God's nature.

- All affirmative prayer and Spiritual Mind Treatment will prevent congested thinking from taking root and allow heaven on your earth to appear in your experiences, if you let it.

- A conscious recognition of the truth will set you free of the untruth. Congestion of the mind is living an untruth.

- The integrity of your mind is dependent on understanding what is in your mind.

- The Infinite Mind is always in action in you. This action of creative ideas is always coming from God.

- God is not interested in the past because God is always a present experience.

Barkerisms
to Take Into Your Everyday Life

The most creative way to live is to be deliberately and consciously anxious to get more knowledge about everything.

- Awakened minds do not retreat and are meant to advance. This is the nature of God's unfoldment throughout the universe and through you.

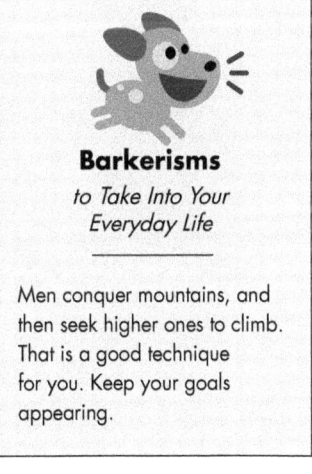

Barkerisms
to Take Into Your Everyday Life

Men conquer mountains, and then seek higher ones to climb. That is a good technique for you. Keep your goals appearing.

- The quickest way to make yourself ill, miserable, or poverty-minded is to have a closed mind.

- You are a spiritual human being. Now that you have become spiritually aware, you can never go back to your inferior thoughts with the same comfort or complacency. Never forget this. Your spiritual creativity is your divine inheritance. It is up to you to use it or not. So Barky asks, "What are you allowing to take root in your mind?"

Am I Ready For a Better Future?

Thinking Spiritually

Dr. Barker said those who "are not afraid of the good, solid mental work of believing" do not expect God to offer them special favors or miracles [in the ordinary expression of life]. These individuals are ready and willing to give great attention to what they want long enough to have the greater experiences in life they desire.

Ask Yourself: What Do I Believe?

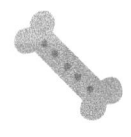

Answer Five Questions to Start Your Journey

1

Do I believe all my highest and best ideas are coming from God or Spirit?

2

Do I believe negative patterns are being discarded by replacing them with better thoughts?

3

Am I ready to accept some really good ideas even if they seem too radical and would change the way I live my life?

4

Do I believe that once I commit myself to a really good idea, the word "impossible" will disappear from my mind?

5

Do I believe practicing spiritual ideas is taking the pressure off of daily living?

Workbook Chapter Summary

E very decision produces a demonstration; this is the most basic and fundamental premise in all of Dr. Barker's writings and public speaking. Ten years prior to the publication of *The Power of Decision, Auntie Mame,* a 1958 movie starring Rosalind Russell, gave birth to a statement that became the hallmark of the title character's fabulous personality. From her magnificent staircase in her penthouse parlor, Auntie Mame declared:

"Life is a banquet and most poor [S-O-Bs] are starving to death!"

As this movie was also a long-standing Broadway show in New York, where Dr. Barker grew his church and large following, we can imagine, no doubt, that he saw it. He would have understood how Auntie Mame saw life and how eagerly she lived it. The movie is an excellent metaphor about being a more vibrant person, one who has figured out how life really works! Living in the light of your own mind and making your own calls in life can serve up a banquet of ideas every day. Dr. Barker made it his life's calling to help others to live well. He declared that to think one person is lucky and another is not is a lie and an alibi. This kind of thinking causes too many people to live only half-heartedly, and, as Auntie Mame opined, "half-starved."

Faltering Minds
Hesitant Minds
Fearful Minds

..... do not give fully
..... exist only half-heartedly
..... and live in the light of other people's minds

Thumbs-Up Barky tells us a real mental housecleaning can have great therapeutic value. By letting go of inferior thinking, old attitudes, biases, and hardened opinions, we stop inviting trouble into our lives.

Our minds are full of great ideas about ourselves that are ready to be acted upon on the day we are born. What we find acceptable as conditions in our mind results in the stories that eventually become our lives. Can we choose a better life? Can we discard old ways? Are we confident that our primary thoughts are truly serving us? These normal questions have become the basis of our journey through this workbook. At this point, we are poised to make a conscious choice and plan for a better future. We have reached some very important decisions in our exercises and assessments. In summary, we have learned a better way to think about ourselves and use spiritual thinking to make and shape our greatest decisions.

Magical Barky shows us that we evolve by moving through form, not by avoiding form, by working with people, not by withdrawing from people.

To see ourselves living consciously opens doors to many future opportunities. Dr. Barker describes this as the new-found freedom of being yourself. And our personal freedom can be the only real security in life. Consciously overseeing our thoughts limits inferior thinking's ability to take root. Even if our life was out of control, seemingly operating without our permission, we now have the ability to make a conscious choice.

Imagine someone who rides around all day with one foot on the gas pedal and one foot on the brake; they have become a worrier. Every day this individual avoids or delays all consequences, most of which they imagine are catastrophic. They can't move forward, sideways or backward. Now imagine that they learn that it's their responsibility to accept new ideas and act upon them. This is what Dr. Barker believed was the normal business of knowing your own mind. Whole results, he explained, can only come from whole thinking. In other words, you can't be half-hearted, timid, or reluctant and expect your benefit to be whole or satisfying. You must do the mental work.

Happy Barky believes our future is not dependent on five years from now. It is what we are now. The future is today projected.

It is recommended that you subscribe to a simple and all-important instruction: move your feet and do a Spiritual Mind Treatment. Do a Treatment to help you pursue a positive idea and then act, taking initiative immediately. Make a conscious choice to direct your energies in a forward motion to support your idea. This mental effort can only produce real and meaningful results. Dr. Barker would urge all his listeners to make certain that they are alive thinkers! At this point in your workbook self-study, a faltering, hesitant, and fearful thought should be avoided. Only a real mental housecleaning can help you avoid half-hearted living.

Baby Barky has learned the direction of your language indicates the direction of your thinking.

Dr. Barker would remind us that all successful persons are using the same Mind: a Universal Mind. He called it the "Mind factor" and said it was available to everyone, in equal shares and proportion. In other words, faults and virtues are created in our own mind. Through your readings and exercises in each chapter, you have been given a level, mental playing field of useful knowledge. You are now better equipped to be aware of what you can change. Each workbook exercise has allowed you to reassess your thoughts. You understand that you can keep those thoughts, change those thoughts, or dispose of them: in any situation, it's you who control it. You have an inexhaustible, orderly system of greater ideas waiting for you, if you allow the inferior thoughts to drop off and fall away.

Quizzical Barky has decided

an idea accepted is an idea demonstrated.

Your mind is part of the Infinite Mind [God], and it will help you in every way to keep your mind uncluttered and free of negatives.

The only people who will be unable to do this are those who choose to remain limited or ignorant of the facts. Remember, Dr. Barker explained that an inferior thinker suffers from frustration as well as complacency. He said these were the only sins and evil an individual could ever face.

Dr. Barker knew that a balanced life included being healthy, having a fulfilling career, being loved, creative, and happy. If you find one of these not working, likely one area of your life is being neglected. Here you can uncover a misuse of your mind or an inferior thought. You have used your mind to make a problem, but now you know a decision can change all that. With each new idea and decision, your life progresses forward. And a forward-looking and optimistic thinker will always find others to join them. All these individuals are waking up to their potential. Now is your time to enter a new generation of thinkers who use spiritual thoughts to awaken their potential each day.

The good you are seeking is also seeking you.

Dr. Ernest Holmes was known to have said, "What you are looking for, you are looking with." Your mind is always patiently waiting for your receptivity and initiative to make a new decision. God is ready to give you life more abundantly when you accept a new idea about yourself. Negative life experiences may have clouded your thinking and thus kept you from finding your goodness. But you don't have to keep fanning those flames! Ask yourself: are there any issues still stressing me out? If so, go back to your Success Tool #2 A-B-C Exercise in the Special Section: Assess Your Personal Readiness to Change.

Every day, you can do mental housecleaning. Make room for healthier and happier patterns of thought. Life is a banquet to enjoy! Remember Auntie Mame and keep her alive in your thoughts. Yours is not a lifetime of blame or limitation; instead you can have a lifetime of self-cognition. You can be aware that you have the power to generate an intelligent response to all your life choices. Your goal is to achieve the best and most perfect expression of a balanced life that is perfect for you! This is a sure sign of healthy thinking.

Accelerate your effectiveness
Stop wasting your inherent genius
Forget about asking others for advice
..... and you will live more fully
..... and you will live whole-heartedly
..... and you will shine by the light of your own mind,
as one with God

Words, Concepts, and Phrases to Practice in Chapter Eight

In a few simple words, write out what each vocabulary word means. Refer to page 10, the vocabulary section, to review and think about what you understand about each definition. The vocabulary has been written carefully and thoughtfully to help you understand spiritual terms, concepts, and practices. A new vocabulary is essential to help you deepen your understanding about what is powering your decision to bring about your desired result. Once you better understand these words and how to use them correctly, you will grow into a more evolved spiritual thinker who gets better results.

Law of Growth:

_____
_____
_____
_____
_____
_____

Spiritual Evolution:

_____
_____
_____
_____
_____
_____
_____

Treatment:

_____
_____
_____
_____
_____
_____
_____

Barky

Additional Impressions and Notes

_____
_____
_____
_____
_____
_____
_____
_____
_____
_____
_____
_____
_____
_____
_____
_____
_____
_____
_____

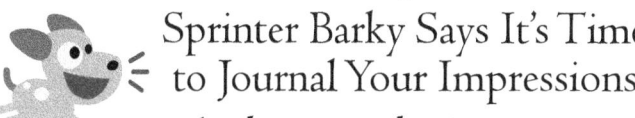

Sprinter Barky Says It's Time to Journal Your Impressions

Accelerate your decisions so you can reach the finish line!

Writing contributes to emotional well-being, increases mental and emotional clarity, reduces stress, and increases problem-solving.

Write down your AH-HA moments, realizations, recognitions, or exclamations of sudden understanding. For example, did any of the five questions cause you to stop and ponder your answers? Did you think back on a specific life choice you made? Did the chapter summary make you think more deeply about a personal goal or decision? Are you considering how you might grow more spiritual? Perhaps one or more AH-HA moments include all of the above! *What has been stirred up inside of you? Write your impressions down here.*

_____

_____

_____

_____

_____

_____

_____

_____

_____

_____

_____

_____

_____

_____

_____

_____

_____

REVIEW EXERCISES *from all 8 chapters*

Let's review those all-important takeaways from your chapter exercises:

You learned your natural birthright is to have

Great health

More wealth

Greater joy

Creative self-expression

Greater abundance

More love

You recognized that you can misuse your mind by

Worrying too much

Being too fearful

Expecting dis-ease as normal

Envying and resenting others

Not being open-minded to new ideas

Being too complacent to change

You assessed your own personal readiness for change.

You asked yourself if you had unclear motivations, or conflicting or competing values, that stopped you from making your decisions. You learned to assess if you had self-limiting thoughts and fears about the unknown. You found out if your emotions are getting stuck in old conversations about past life events.

You used two simple success tools to remove those negative thoughts and beliefs about your life.

Success Tool #1

You changed "I can't" to "I won't":

I can't find time to diet. ➡ *I won't take time to diet.*

I can't use social media because it's too complicated. ➡ *I won't use social media because it's not a good use of my time.*

Success Tool #2

*You learned that a new **A-B-C** conversation can remove negative feelings. When you have a new "**B**" conversation with yourself you can tell yourself something new about events of the past. A new "**B**" conversation today allows you to change your "**C**" pattern of strong emotions about those past events, freeing you to move on to new and happier life experiences.*

You learned that indecision is your decision to fail.

- Your health will be impaired when you regard disease as normal.

- Your wealth will be compromised by fearing the worst in financial affairs.

- Your joy can be muted by overly concentrating on your failures.

- Your perfect self-expression fades easily when you fall back into competitive or comparative thinking instead of original thinking.

- Living richly should not rely on your past lifestyles or experiences.

- New hopes about love can be overshadowed by doubts and believing it can't happen to you.

Thumbs Up Barky says you can stop patterns of indecision by making new decisions about what you want instead of focusing on what you don't want.

You learned that the creative process awaits your decision to bring about all the perfect results you desire.

You learned that no one is better informed or equipped to determine your good than you are!

You learned to write out the steps of a Spiritual Mind Treatment. These steps give you the right spiritual framework to think c-o-r-r-e-c-t-l-y. You generate new decisions to live richly and be happy, healthy, and creative when you commit to these five steps:

Step 1: YOU realize that there is only one God.

Step 2: YOU unify yourself with that loving God and Its Mind and Intelligence.

Step 3: YOU declare some good you want for yourself and place it into God's care.

Step 4: YOU express genuine gratitude for the good before the demonstration.

Step 5: YOU release your Treatment, expecting a demonstration through the Law of Growth operating within the Universal Mind.

And you conclude every Treatment with **"And so it is!"**

You learned about the Circles of Thought and how to make more WOW Decisions in your life!

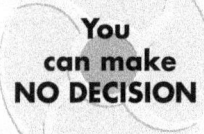

| You can make NO DECISION | Or feel pressure to make a NOW DECISION | Or learn how to make a WOW DECISION |

You learned that theological concepts are not the same as spiritual understanding. Clear spiritual thinking can help you achieve spiritual understanding in all areas of your life!

THEOLOGICAL CONCEPTS	SPIRITUAL UNDERSTANDING
God is a Super Man.	God is a creative and Universal Intelligence.
God giveth and taketh away.	God gives itself away by means of me.
God is a spiritual mystery that cannot be comprehended or understood.	I operate as an individualization of the One Mind, and I experience Its presence in me as God's ideas in action.
God will think me worthy someday in the future or afterlife.	My Treatment affirms my oneness and worthiness to receive my good from a loving God that is present in me now.

You learned that Comparison Thinking creates a **NO DECISION.**

You learned that Competitive Thinking requires a **NOW DECISION.**

You learned that Original Thinking produces a **WOW DECISION!**

You learned there is no quicker way to make yourself miserable, ill, and poverty-minded than to have a closed mind.

SO WHAT'S IN YOUR MIND?

Qualities of a CLOSED MIND

Being mentally/physically congested

Stuck in old ruts, with NO decisions

Resigned to situations you believe impossible to get out of

Mental calcification

Qualities of an OPEN MIND

Relying on self-fulfilling mental action

Willingness to fast from all negatives

Living under a law of mental expansion and belief your God is always available

Not being afraid of new spiritual ideas

EXERCISE THREE: PREPARING MY GREATEST DECISION OF ALL - TO LIVE ON THE SIDE OF GREATNESS

First, write out some descriptive words that best describe your thoughts and ideas.

Descriptive words that help you recognize a God that is present:

_____
_____

Descriptive words that unify you with a present and loving God:

_____
_____

Your description of some particular good you want and desire NOW:

_____ _____
_____

Your words of gratitude that best describe how you feel in the present:

_____
_____

What you want to say to release your Treatment, placing your intention into God's care:

_____
_____

My Treatment to Experience My Own Unique Greatness

DATE WRITTEN:_____ /_____ /_____

_____
_____
_____
_____
_____
_____
_____
_____
_____
_____

I RELEASE MY TREATMENT TO A LOVING GOD AND SO IT IS!

Takeaways to Raise Your Consciousness Now and Forever

Simplified Overview of All Eight Chapters

There is no way to sum up all the wisdom in Dr. Barker's writings, but we can reflect upon what we have learned. Pick several things that are meaningful to you and apply them over and over again to bring about new results in your life. Begin now to practice the mental discipline to place spiritual awareness ahead of all your decisions.

Decisions are a choice: they are a recipe for living. An awakened, spiritual attitude will always require periodic mental housecleaning. Our acceptance of new ideas shows our willingness to have an open mind. Why not choose on the side of your own greatness every day? Why not have a fuller life uniquely your own? Isn't it time to start using the power of decision every day to awaken to all your life's rewards?

Here are some of the most important concepts to remember:

CHAPTER ONE: You were born in a universe of Intelligence. You have a personality unique to you that was meant to unfold, evolve, and create as that Intelligence.

CHAPTER TWO: Your mind and your emotions are the greatest tools to help you live a balanced life.

CHAPTER THREE: The most important person in life to determine your good is you! God works through you to produce all your greatest results.

CHAPTER FOUR: The only way to change your experience is to become a changed individual. Following this mental and spiritual law will lead you to all your heart's desires.

 **CHAPTER FIVE:** Tomorrow is today amplified. What you think about today is a clue to what you can expect tomorrow.

 CHAPTER SIX: If you neglect healthy attitudes you won't be healthy. The ideas and concepts you accept in your mind today are primary to successful and meaningful living tomorrow.

 **CHAPTER SEVEN:** Spiritual thinking will help you think correctly and open up an Intelligent Universe for your daily use. Your conscious mind was created to be used to explore new ideas that are right for you and decide which ones will take priority and lead you to success.

 CHAPTER EIGHT: Indecision is a valley you can half-heartedly live in the rest of your life. Or you can take authority over your own mind and emotions and have great mountaintop experiences. The choice is yours.

Dr. Raymond Charles Barker:

His Quest to Teach Proven Spiritual Practices

A Contemporary Perspective on
His Life and the New
Thought Movement

His Quest to Teach Proven Spiritual Practices

"We can stop the unintelligent factors from taking over our lives," declared Dr. Raymond Charles Barker, who devoted all his talks, lectures, books, and articles to the subject. His passion to help people use the power of decision became the focus of his healing ministry. His insistence on sharing his spiritual method of personal change led to the 1968 publication of one of his most popular books, *The Power of Decision*, and it remains in publication five decades later. This workbook, written to inspire and help new generations, encourages all audiences to use these practical methods and spiritual concepts to achieve greater, personal success.

Dr. Barker (1911-1988) emphasized in all his lectures and books that it was essential to know that a creative Law of Mind will demonstrate results from individual thoughts. His work helped thousands of people to let go of their attachment to inferior thoughts that lead to poor results. He believed using spiritual practices enriched peoples' lives and led to greater ideas about themselves and more abundant living. He gave people hope for a new day. He encouraged, even challenged, his audiences to move beyond self-control. He believed self-imposed prohibitions only made people suffer needlessly. He told his audiences that their souls were not suffering from the judgmental acts of an unloving God, but from their own inferior thinking. An intelligent Universal Mind [God] did not intend its creation to suffer. Barker's popular message was that this loving, intelligent Universal Mind was available to everyone. He along with other New Thought practitioners of the 20th and 21st centuries believed ideas are discovered through a natural conscious relationship with a Universal Mind. Our personal access to this Mind was a discovery that needed to be taught to the world.

Throughout his lifetime, Dr. Barker was a popular speaker, alongside the likes of Napoleon Hill, Rev. Dr. Norman Vincent Peale, Rev. Billy Graham, Dale Carnegie, Emmet Fox, Maxwell Maltz M.D., Zig Ziglar, and Rev. Ike Eisenhower. Later Wayne Dyer Ph.D., Tony Robbins, Louise Hay, Jean Houston, Julia Cameron, and Marianne Williamson, to name a few, would popularize his message and re-frame his spiritual concepts into their own voice. Many who know these and other names should also know they were students and followers of Dr. Barker, as well as early adopters of New Thought concepts and practices.

New Thought for Modern Problems

As an author, teacher, and minister, Dr. Barker spoke regularly to the spiritually liberal generations of his time. In his heyday, he broadcast his message on 22 radio stations from Lincoln Center in New York City. The singular goal of his message was to heal the whole planet of inferior attitudes and behaviors. He wanted everyone to know they could independently initiate enormous personal change if they adopted a spiritual model to guide their choices.

In a fast-paced society, Dr. Barker and other New Thought teachers from around the world offered courses and counsel to individuals, groups, and organizations, helping them to use spiritual principles in all matters of health, career, success, and relationship building. These practitioners believed these spiritual concepts were fundamental to a balanced life. Growing and diverse populations of people were looking for new ways to advance their minds. Business and industry were demanding more skilled decision-makers for a new century. New Thought teachers understood their time had come to spiritually equip and counsel individuals in the use of spiritual concepts and best practices. They held a vision for how a modern society could solve many problems, including poverty, divorce, escalating health issues, brok n homes, and failed careers, which they believed were all extensions of poverty thinking. Any belief system popularized in society or religious circles that led people to believe external forces were always withholding their good was a lie and an abhorrence to a New Thought Practitioner.

For additional study of the historical foundations of New Thought denominations, please refer to Unity Practical School of Christianity, Religious Science, Christian Science, and Divine Science. Dr. Barker also became well known in the growing study of spiritual psychology. With Dr. Maxwell Maltz, M.D., he coauthored *Conquest of Frustration*. Dr. Maltz is best known for his book, *Psycho Cybernetics*. Both were early adopters of spiritual concepts to help people with behavioral challenges.

A Case for Spirituality and Natural Law to Aid Decision-Makers

Although New Thought was finding new audiences in America, it actually had arrived much earlier in the mid-1850s and abroad. In Europe and elsewhere, the concept that a spiritual science could make the case for a material cause and effect to explain how our demonstrations [results in life] occur was frequently discussed and debated in many formal and informal circles. Dr. Barker, among other prominent thinkers, studied theology, psychology, and philosophy, and wanted the world to see spiritual thinking as an extension of a natural and universal law of cause and effect. He believed every individual could be taught to understand this. If people were given a practical understanding of why the whole Universe worked intelligently and creatively on their thoughts, they would be emboldened to use their minds more wisely [while on earth].

He and other New Thought Practitioners wanted their audiences to dispense with the belief that a judgmental God was on a throne. They wanted people to stop believing that God was forever punishing them for past mistakes, thus rendering them unworthy of God's love and acceptance. If given an understanding of natural laws, people could recover from all inferior thinking and move toward more vibrant living.

New Thought Practitioners made the case that spiritual thinking coexisted with the laws of science and nature. As one of these Practitioners, Dr. Barker believed that we could explain our demonstrations; they were the logical result of some conscious or unconscious decision we made. This led to additional applications of New Thought in support of human development and human performance.

The notion that each person was an individualization of an Intelligent, Universal Mind that was running the universe was a novel one to teach. But more importantly this working relationship between the minds of man and God was also a practical solution to growing questions about the causes of social and personal ills. Currently, several hundred of Dr. Barker's lectures are being digitized for future audiences and people interested in personal growth around the world.

The Expansion of Personal Discovery and Recovery Programs Around the World

His lectures, books, and articles led to a broader acceptance of New Thought in new circles of society. Gradually, as these new audiences were cultivated, modern society saw the relevance of his consciousness-raising methods to the emerging fields of sports training, mental health and wellness programming, and other popularized, self-improvement courses and methods.

New secular audiences from sales executives, professional organizations, and corporate boardrooms to fraternal orders and community-based service organizations sought out more positive ways to create leaders for all types of initiatives. Many listened regularly to Dr. Barker's talks and lectures broadcast throughout the country. We are fortunate he left a publishing legacy that would later become a cornerstone of the New Thought movement.

Born and raised in Rochester, New York, he was introduced at an early age to Unity Christian teachings. In 1939, he was ordained as a Minister. After graduating from the Unity School of Practical Christianity in Lee's Summit Missouri, Rev. Barker later received his Doctor of Divinity following his affiliation with Dr. Ernest Holmes, the Founder of Religious Science in Los Angeles, California. Dr. Barker was drawn to Dr. Holmes for his early contributions to and development of "scientific prayer." This scientific method of prayer would later be called Spiritual Mind Treatment. Dr. Holmes, author of the 1938 classic textbook *The Science of Mind*, eagerly called upon Rev. Barker in 1946 to open the First Church of Religious Science in New York City. At the time, Dr. Barker was serving as the President of the International New Thought Alliance (INTA). He would later go on to serve two terms as President of Religious Science International, an expanding association of churches that practiced and taught Spiritual Mind healing throughout the country.

Known today as Centers for Spiritual Living, these New Thought churches and centers continue to expand in the U.S. and globally. These centers teach and practice the practical methods of Spiritual Mind healing, with Spiritual Mind Treatment as a daily practice. For further information visit, *scienceofmind.com* or *CSL.org*. Additional resources include *newthoughtalliance.org*, *unity.org* and *findacenter.com*.

How to Assess Your Readiness to Change

As we strive to do better in our lives, we may put up resistance to change our present circumstances, even if the outcome is better for us. See how your thoughts, words, and memories can stand between you and greater success.

Assess Your
Personal Readiness to Change

Now that you have identified inferior thoughts that are unhealthy to keep holding onto, it is time to look at how willing you are to let go of them. By identifying those reoccurring thoughts that keep you negatively charged, you have discovered potential roadblocks for greater living. Sometimes these negatively-charged thoughts act like internal brakes or resistance factors impeding you from a fuller expression of life as described on p. 26. Take this opportunity to look within. Look from a psychological level to assess the influence your experiences have had on developing your emotional reactions to life's events.

What is Living in the Zone?

In the many ways Dr. Federer coached individuals for greater success and even star performance, she found people often had to overcome their resistance to change first. Once you start to understand the origins of resistance, you can begin to do something about it. She says there are 4 Points of Resistance to Change to watch out for:

Point 1 Unclear motivations
Point 2 Conflicting values or competing values
Point 3 Self-limiting thoughts and beliefs about yourself and the world
Point 4 Emotions like fear of the unknown or a natural tendency to avoid pain and discomfort (*Working in the Zone*, p.33)

What Are Some of the Ways I Could Be Resisting Change?

Let's take a deeper dive into Dr. Federer's 4 Points of Resistance from the previous page.

Have you ever had any of these conversations with yourself?

Point 1 Unclear motivation Would I lose the support of my family if I move to a different city? Can I be sure I will succeed if I take this new job? Do I trust in the advice my doctor has given me?

Point 2 Conflicting values or competing values If I complain to my boss, will my co-workers think I am disloyal? If I say something to my husband about his drinking, will he think I don't love him? If I leave off my resume that I got fired from a job, am I still being honest?

Barkerisms
to Take Into Your Everyday Life

Complacency is an evil [negative suggestion]. It has no place in the creative process. When it enthralls your mind, subconscious trouble begins.

Point 3 Self-limiting thoughts and beliefs about yourself or the world around you Everyone thinks if you are over 65, you are over-the-hill. Who would really care if I lose 50 pounds? I don't have enough experience to apply for a manager's job I desire. There are so many more people in the world who deserve this opportunity more than me.

Point 4 Emotions like fear of the unknown or a natural tendency to avoid pain and discomfort My doctor says it's a new procedure, but I'll wait until more people have gone through it. I don't want to wear a mask, so no I don't think I will fly and take that vacation trip. I just don't like exercise, so what's a few extra pounds?

Using other examples on the following page, see how many ways resistance can show up in subtle and not-so-subtle ways. Make a review of your thoughts, concerns, and emotions. Could you be neglecting some area of your life without realizing it?

Examples of How Resistance Can Show Up in Your Next Steps

Let's see how these 4 Points of Resistance can cause us to second guess ourselves, be afraid, or even lie to ourselves and others.

These examples are taken from Chapter One, Exercises 1 – 3

Example of Point 1: Do I have an unclear motivation for adding more nutrition to all my meals? Do I really want to change how I cook for myself? How will my family react when I start cooking different foods? Will they support me doing this or argue with me we should go back to our old ways?

Example of Point 2: Do I have conflicting or competing values that would interfere with my having a quiet space to meditate? Do I really want to reorganize my personal space for quiet meditation? This could be a problem since we don't have a big home. I don't know how my husband would feel If I created my own "woman cave" and made him move his stuff out of our spare room.

Example of Point 3: Do I possess any self-limiting thoughts or beliefs that prevent me from walking 30 minutes each day? I realize now that I am afraid to walk alone. I think women are targets. I am not sure my neighbors would even walk with me. I don't know them well.

Example of Point 4: Do I go out of my way to avoid pain and discomfort spending so much on credit cards? If I don't have a budget, I can't blow it. Right? I'll just buy this for myself now and give it to myself for Christmas later; no one will know. I'll just pay a little each month to stay on budget and not tell my husband about the growing balance.

On the following pages write down what is causing you to resist. What conversations could you be having with yourself?

Quizzical Barky asks, "Are you sure inferior thinking hasn't gotten in the way of real progress?"

Refer to your own goals and next steps from Page 34, Chapter One, Exercise 3, and write out what could get in the way of making these important changes in your life. If you wish to update a life area or add a new step, now is a good time to make these changes here.

IMPORTANT FOR ME TO DO_____
Life Area to Improve

What are your top three next steps?

Step _____

Step _____

Step _____

How are the 4 Points of Resistance showing up to prevent you from taking your next steps?

Point 1: Do I have an unclear motivation for taking this step?

_____

_____

_____

Point 2: Do I have conflicting or competing values that could interfere with my making changes?

_____

_____

_____

Point 3: Do I possess self-limiting thoughts or beliefs that prevent me from proceeding with confidence?

_____

_____

_____

Point 4: What tendency to avoid pain or discomfort would interfere with me moving forward?

_____

_____

_____

IMPORTANT FOR ME TO DO_____
Life Area to Improve

What are your top three next steps?

Step _____

Step _____

Step _____

How are the 4 Points of Resistance showing up to prevent you from taking your next steps?

Point 1: Do I have an unclear motivation for taking this step?

_____

_____

_____

Point 2: Do I have conflicting or competing values that could interfere with my making a change?

_____

_____

Point 3: Do I possess self-limiting thoughts or beliefs that would prevent me from proceeding?

_____

_____

_____

Point 4: What tendency to avoid pain or discomfort would interfere with moving forward?

_____

_____

_____

_____

_____

IMPORTANT FOR ME TO DO _____
Life Area to Improve

What are your top three next steps?

Step _____

Step _____

Step _____

How are the 4 Points of Resistance showing up to prevent you from taking your next steps?

Point 1: Do I have an unclear motivation for taking this step?

_____

_____

_____

Point 2: Do I have conflicting or competing values that could interfere with making a change?

_____

_____

_____

Point 3: Do I possess self-limiting thoughts or beliefs that would prevent me from proceeding?

_____

_____

_____

Point 4: What tendency to avoid pain or discomfort would interfere with moving forward?

_____

_____

_____

_____

USE THESE TWO SIMPLE TOOLS TO REMOVE NEGATIVE THOUGHTS OR BELIEFS

The incredible power of your mind has much to do with how you are psychologically motivated to behave. When you want to make a change in your behavior, keep it simple—key in on what you are thinking about routinely. Let's see how Dr. Barker's spiritual goals for successful decisions can be accelerated by doing this self-analysis in the ZONE as presented by Dr. Federer.

WHAT WE TELL OURSELVES MATTERS

DECONSTRUCTIVE THOUGHT	CORE BELIEF	CONSTRUCTIVE THOUGHT
When our optimism is low and we become very pessimistic, we tell ourselves, "The future looks bleak or I see no future."	OPTIMISM is a strong predictor of success.	When we have a high level of optimism, we tell ourselves, "I am excited about the future."

During a time of constructive thinking, our belief convinces us to act on or even change our behavior. So when we believe there is plenty of good to go around for everyone and we are worthy of receiving this good for ourselves, we are being constructive. Constructive thinking enhances the power of all our decisions.

Baby Barky says, "Keep it simple when learning new words."

Go to the next page to start using these tools! A simple change in the words you say to yourself can change your motivation.

Tool #1:
Change "I Can't" to "I Won't"

When you make a conscious choice of words, you increase your ability to be in control and not just allow any circumstance to evolve. However, there are times when we make passive word choices instead of active ones. These passive thoughts can result in a misuse of your mind, your thoughts, and emotions, leading to frustration and unsatisfying results. So Barky asks, "What's in your mind?"

Dr. Federer suggests we can embrace our personal power by shifting our mental framework from…

"I can't do something"
to
"I won't do something"

When you say "I can't," it suggests you are not capable of doing whatever follows that phrase. You diminish yourself and rob yourself of power each time you utter it. (Federer, *Working in the Zone*, p.75).

"I can't"   Implies you are powerless and blaming someone or something else for your missed opportunity.

"I won't"   Says you are perfectly capable but have made the decision not to do something. Saying "I won't" means you are taking full responsibility for the outcome.

Examples for your review

Tool #1 Worksheet

"I can't"	"I won't"
(Implies you are powerless)	(Says you are capable)
I can't find clothes that fit me.	*I won't take time to travel across town to shop for myself.*
I can't use social media. It is just too complicated.	*I won't use social media because I don't believe it is a good use of my time.*
I can't find time to diet and exercise.	*I won't take time to diet right now because I have too many social obligations through the holidays.*
I can't get a pay increase because they are only hiring younger people to do the same work I do.	*I won't spend time to rewrite my resume. I don't believe my work experience will be valued.*
I can't make it to the 12-Step program because I don't get off until 5 p.m.	*I won't go into the 12-Step meeting because I am too afraid I might see someone I know.*
I can't cook so why invite friends over?	*I don't know how to cook the recipes I know my friends would like.*
I can't see why I should color my hair or get clothes that fit me better; nobody is looking anyway.	*I won't spend the money on myself to improve my looks.*

Use Tool #1 to Live With Greater Purpose

TO IMPROVE MY PHYSICAL AND MENTAL HEALTH

Change: I can't:_____ to: I won't:_____

_____ _____

Change: I can't:_____ to: I won't:_____

_____ _____

TO IMPROVE MY RELATIONSHIP WITH MONEY

Change: I can't:_____ to: I won't:_____

_____ _____

Change: I can't:_____ to: I won't:_____

_____ _____

TO BE MORE CREATIVE AND SELF-EXPRESSIVE

Change: I can't:_____ to: I won't:_____

_____ _____

Change: I can't:_____ to: I won't:_____

_____ _____

TO INCREASE MY CAREER
OPTIONS / AVOCATIONAL INTERESTS

Change: I can't:_____ to: I won't:_____

_____ _____

Change: I can't:_____ to: I won't:_____

_____ _____

TO FIND MORE JOY IN MY LIFE

Change: I can't:_____ to: I won't:_____

_____ _____

Change: I can't:_____ to: I won't:_____

_____ _____

TO EXPERIENCE MORE LOVE IN MY LIFE

Change: I can't:_____ to: I won't:_____

_____ _____

Change: I can't:_____ t o: I won't:_____

_____ _____

What you tell yourself increases your motivation to act, think, and behave differently. What direction are your thoughts taking you?

After completing this simple exercise, you can now see the benefits of having different conversations with yourself and others. Saying "I won't" will help you stop making untrue statements and concealing your true feelings. This helps you and helps others too!

Tool #2: *What You Tell Yourself Really Does Matter*

Another simple and effective way to minimize inferior thoughts and words is to use this **A-B-C** Model. Dr. Federer says that in order to change how you think and feel about a past event, you first have to modify your beliefs. What you tell yourself over and over again, good or bad, can affect your happiness, health, joy, and creative self-expression.

Inner conversations can get negatively charged in a cycle of negative thinking. We get stuck by reliving old hurts over and over again, often to painful and unsatisfying ends. Use this simple **A-B-C** Tool to change those internal conversations and stop the cycle of unproductive thinking.

Don't think that you can control events. But know that you can live and die daily by your reactions to them.

A	B	C
An event occurred in my life	*I have thoughts and beliefs about that event*	*I reacted with strong feelings about that event*
A is NEUTRAL; it happened, and it is a fact. The event did occur; it is true so far as the facts go.	What I tell myself about the event is the most important thing I do. This conversation I have with myself traps me in a perpetual cycle of loss if I don't understand there is a part **C**—my reactions and feelings. I could get stuck and remain at step **B** forever. Events **A** will come and go throughout my life, but a new **B** plus **C** allows me to release and let go of old feelings and move on with new life experiences.	Your reactions and feelings are generated by what you told yourself (**B**) about the event. The event **A** is always a NEUTRAL occurrence. You can change **C** if and only if you entertain an updated **B** conversation with yourself.

REMEMBER: **A**, the event, does not cause **C**, your reactions and feelings. **B**, what you told yourself about the event, makes **C** occur. **B** always gives birth to **C**. So are you prepared to reassess **B**, your thoughts and beliefs, to have a different conversation with yourself today? In order to change your negatively charged **C** feelings about the event, you must update your **B** conversation. If you can have a new **B** conversation with yourself today, then you are ready to release those negatively charged feelings and emotions from your life and move forward with more joy. **Try using the worksheets on the next pages.**

Tool #2: A-B-C Worksheet 1
How to Change Your Life With
a New "B" Conversation

Think back to a situation that upset you. Identify clearly this event **A** in your mind. Let's see what you told yourself **(B)** back then. Could you imagine telling yourself something different today, a new **B**, that would shed new light on that situation? Could you tell yourself something different that would allow you to release that painful memory or lessen its impact on you? Try this exercise with several events using Worksheets 2 and 3 on the following pages. Feel your feelings and really listen to what you could say differently to yourself.

So what happened? What was event **A**? _____

_____

What feelings did you have about that event **(C)**? _____

_____

How would you rate this event in your life?

1 ◄———————————— **5** ————————► **10**
Mildly upsetting   *Very upsetting*

Think back. At the time, what thoughts did you tell yourself about that event? **(B)**_____

_____

What new conversation could you have with yourself today **(B)** about that event **(A)** that would change your feelings or reaction **(C)**? Rewrite your new **B**: _____

_____

Are you prepared to see that your feelings and reactions **(C)** could be different with a new conversation **(B)**? Write your new **C** feelings and emotions: _____

_____

_____

Tool #2: A-B-C Worksheet 2
How to Change Your Life With
a New "B" Conversation

Think back to a situation that upset you. Identify clearly this event **A** in your mind. Let's see what you told yourself (**B**) back then. Could you imagine telling yourself something differently today, a new **B**, that would shed new light on that situation? Could you tell yourself something different that would allow you to release that painful memory or lessen its impact on you? Try this exercise with several events. Feel your feelings and really listen to what you could say differently to yourself today.

So what happened? What was event **A**? _____

_____

What feelings did you have about that event (**C**)? _____

_____

How would you rate this event in your life?

1 ◀━━━━━━━━━ **5** ━━━━━━━━━▶ **10**
Mildly upsetting   *Very upsetting*

Think back. At the time, what thoughts did you tell yourself about that event? **B**:_____

_____

What new conversation could you have with yourself today (**B**) about that event (**A**) that would change your feelings or reaction (**C**)? Rewrite your new **B**: _____

_____

Are you prepared to see that your feelings and reactions (**C**) could be different with a new conversation (**B**)? Write your new **C** feelings and emotions: _____

_____

Tool #2: A-B-C Worksheet 3
How to Change Your Life With
a New "B" Conversation

Think back about a situation that upset you. Identify clearly this event
A in your mind. Let's see what you told yourself (**B**) back then. Could
you imagine telling yourself something differently today, a new **B**,
that would shed new light on that situation? Could you tell yourself
something different that would allow you to release that painful memory
or lessen its impact on you? Try this exercise with several events. Feel
your feelings and really listen to what you could say differently to
yourself today.

So what happened? What was event **A**? _____

_____

What feelings did you have about that event (**C**)? _____

_____

How would you rate this event in your life?

1 ⟵⟶ **5** ⟵⟶ **10**

Mildly upsetting   *Very upsetting*

Think back. At the time, what thoughts did you tell yourself about that
event? **B**:_____

_____

What new conversation could you have with yourself today (**B**) about
that event **A** that would change your feelings or reaction (**C**)? Rewrite
your new **B**: _____

_____

Are you prepared to see that your feelings and reactions (**C**) could be
different with a new conversation **B**? Write your new **C** feelings and
emotions: _____

_____

Summing Up Your Opportunities to Be in the Zone

Whether you want to become a better parent or a more successful sales executive you must first be willing to assess your behavior and change as needed. "The ability to embrace change and do things differently is the key to achieving your goals and becoming a Star Performer." (Federer, *Working In the Zone*, p.26) Being "In the Zone" is often described like this:

- Feeling completely at one with what you are doing

- Feeling able to control your destiny

- Being in a state of consciousness where you are fully absorbed with what you are doing, to the exclusion of all other thoughts

- Bringing your mind and body together to work effortlessly to perform a skill or task, also known as flow

Being in the Zone Applies to Your Spiritual Thinking Too!

You have discovered that your mind and emotions can consciously or unconsciously obstruct and compromise the enjoyment you get out of life. Assessing your thoughts and behaviors from the past is a big step in achieving greater awareness about how to construct future conversations with yourself. When you seek the benefits of "working in the Zone" to recover from inferior thinking such as worry and fear, you will greatly enhance your motivation to change. Once you have used these tools to reduce your resistance to change, you can move forward with greater ease and grace in all areas of your life.

Here are 4 guiding principles to take you to a higher level of spiritual thinking:

Principle 1 The universe you live in is orderly and always acts and reacts intelligently to your thoughts. You can experience a high quality of life in these areas:

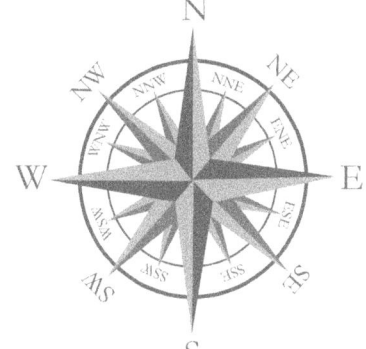

- *Your Health*
- *Your Wealth / Money*
- *Your Joy*
- *Your Self-Expression / Evolution*
- *Your Career / Avocation*
- *Your Love*

Principle 2 This Universe is intelligent, creative, and serves as a purposeful framework for life to coexist. Knowing there is a creative process in you adds to your capacity to make more intelligent decisions. Any creation by an Infinite Intelligence, which is what you are, would have to be intelligent. Your birthright is to think intelligently.

Principle 3 The creative and orderly Universe is never indecisive, never disturbed, and never defeated by your past experiences. Your only limits in life are found in the acceptance of an inferior thought. An individual may demonstrate a limited thought, but the universe is never limited by that thought.

Principle 4 There is one God, one Mind, one Cause, and one Intelligence, and you are It at the individual level; it is your personality expressed. You are given this totality of intelligence for your use and your distribution of great ideas in your life. Many wonderful demonstrations will occur if you will accept there is a universal power that is actively present in the unfoldment of all your decisions.

Now, return to page 36 to complete Chapter One Review.

Mountaineer Barky Says It's Time to Journal Your Impressions

Can you see yourself going to a higher level of spiritual thinking?

Writing contributes to emotional well-being, increases mental and emotional clarity, reduces stress, and increases problem-solving.

Write down your AH-HA moments, realizations, recognitions, or exclamations of sudden understanding. Perhaps one or more AH-HA moments include all of the above! *What has been stirred up inside of you? Write your impressions down here.*

How to Give Yourself a Spiritual Mind Treatment in Five Proven Steps

A Contemporary Way to Pray
Affirmatively and Intelligently
to Put the Answer in
Every Prayer

Spiritual Mind Treatment

"The real self is God and as such is to be implicitly trusted."

Dr. Ernest Holmes, creator of the Scientific Method of Prayer

Everyone can use this scientific approach to prayer. Treatment is based on a science of prayer, a method of proven success [answered prayer] rather than the more traditional supplication to a far-off Deity [Anthropomorphic Being]. Spiritual Mind Treatment is the way to pray effectively, always placing the answer in the prayer and to a God who is present. "We are all divine inlets to God," stated poet and essayist Ralph Waldo Emerson. When your mental inlet to God is blocked with inferior thoughts, possibly put there in error, you need to clear out those blockages.

"Most people pray to a God who is not present. They are between the 'haves' and 'have nots' in life," explains Dr. Lloyd George Tupper, a student of Dr. Barker and a Ministerial colleague of Dr. Ernest Holmes, who had the profound insight to propose Spiritual Mind Treatment and the steps that accompanied it. Insisting God is always present and ready to give us Its [God's] best ideas, Dr. Holmes stated that an effective Treatment must always be independent of any existing circumstance. Each of the 5 steps of Treatment are meant to lift you above the contemplation of conditions [feeling unworthy or poor in circumstance] and help you mentally believe that God stands ready to help you now.

Treatment affirmatively makes all things new in your experience [your demonstrations] through a Law of Growth. Refer to *Treat Yourself to Life*, another book by Dr. Barker, as well as *365 Days of Richer Living*, a book coauthored by Dr. Ernest Holmes and Dr. Barker, both of which offer numerous examples of Treatments for different situations.

How Treatment Differs from Traditional Prayer

FIRST: It stirs up a spiritual presence within you right now.

Spiritual Mind Treatment is a personal and direct way to speak to God. God is always present in your life. You are the individual vessel through which the Treatment is delivered and made a conscious choice, a deliberate action, and a direct pathway to the living presence of the God within you. As mental preparation, you become emotionally peaceful and at ease before you speak. This will help you be a better listener to your own thoughts and God's ideas for you.

SECOND: It removes the duality of thinking that there is a heaven and a physical earth. In Treatment, you recognize that God's presence is right where you are and not in some fanciful location.

To the degree you allow it, you were born to experience heaven on earth. Listen deeply for God's greater ideas for you. You must make it your goal to act on those ideas. This can be difficult for people who want instant miracles. When you speak your word, you are directing the Intelligence of a loving God to some desired result. You act with a belief in that Intelligence; you accept your unification with It right in the midst of your affirmative prayer.

Treatment as a spiritually correct process removes this dual sense that there is a heaven and a physical earth where everyone toils to prove their worth to God. Through Treatment, you are no longer praying to a God in a heavenly mansion. God is with you now and gives you Its Intelligence and unique ideas to solve your problems and move you one step closer to achieving all your heart's desires, the desired goals you were born to fulfill.

THIRD: Your words focus exclusively on what you want: love, joy, and happiness, the health and creative expression you aspire to, and your greatest career choice and pathway. All of these are necessary to the balanced life that God wants for you on earth.

In Treatment, you are never begging God to give you things. God is always in a present state of expectancy. It always acts as a receiving Mind, receptive to your thoughts. God cannot refuse your good or refuse to accept your ideas. God makes no judgment on your inferior thoughts. Of utmost importance, ask for what you want, and don't feel like you are taking away from anyone's dreams, resources, and goals. Your goals in life should be more than just getting your needs met. Treatment is about your heart's desires and is meant to always raise your thoughts above the basic level of your everyday needs.

FOURTH: It clarifies what God is and is doing in your life.

You personify the qualities of God to the extent that you realize that you are an individualization of God while on earth. Know that the Intelligence [God] that created the physical universe is the same Intelligence that created you. You, the individual, are how God expresses itself. Its [God's] work can only be done through you! Treatment is practicing daily your total acceptance of this unification. An experience of the presence of God is WHAT YOU NEED everyday and throughout life!

Don't let your inner brilliance stay hidden because of confused ideas about what God is or is not doing in your life. Everything you put into your Treatment is in God's care. BELIEVE IT all the way to your next greatest decision!

Now let's turn to the five steps of Treatment as described by Dr. Holmes and learn how to put them into practice.

5 STEPS TO GIVE YOURSELF A SPIRITUAL MIND TREATMENT

Step 1: RECOGNIZE that there is only one God.

Begin your Treatment by stating that there is only one God, one Universal Mind, and this Mind is your mind. Treatment is a reverent acknowledgment of what God is doing in your life. Its presence is known to you the moment you speak your first word. Think of yourself as stirring up the living presence of God right now. Each word initiates your access to your higher, spiritual nature, which is God. Step 1 begins the process of praying c-o-r-r-e-c-t-l-y.

Step 2: UNIFY yourself with God.

Say you are an individualization of the Mind of God and are thinking with It right now. As you sense and feel this oneness, you are expressed perfectly. Remind yourself that God can only know Itself through you. The Bible promises that it is God's good pleasure that you have Its Life and have it more abundantly. God and you are always of one accord. Treatment acknowledges this. It is an open expression of a desire for a perfectly expressed life as God would have it for you.

Step 3: Make your DECLARATION of some good you want for yourself or another.

Each word you speak now is a personal declaration of some good you desire. You want something more for yourself and your situation. You thirst to experience your heart's desire. God will not be thrifty in Its demonstration. God does not take from someone else to achieve a higher good for you. In fact, through Treatment you will come to know your good has never been withheld from you. So this is not the time to expect less, but to expect more. This is why most traditional prayers are not answered: the person praying does not put the answer in the prayer. The science of Treatment is "your acceptance of the answer" in the present request, knowing it is in God's care right now. God does not exist to give you things but to give you Its greater ideas to act upon. The good you are seeking is already seeking you. Be ready to receive God's greater ideas when they are whispered in your ears. Listen carefully.

If more love is desired, say this: I know the truth about myself and my heart's desire. I am attracting a loving partnership with the perfect person who is right for me. I can trust myself to know when it is right, whole, and perfect. The joy and happiness I desire are increased by this loving relationship. I accept all the good coming to me because it is being revealed through me and my experiences. This new relationship as it unfolds is meeting my need for a greater expression of love in my life.

If better health is desired, say this: With perfect ease of movement I go about my day. My body knows what to do under every circumstance. With grace I carry myself forward into my daily activities, which are always beneficial to me. I understand what my body needs, and I act on this knowledge to make wise choices. I act on the ideas of God to experience greater health in many beneficial and new ways. Any negative thoughts about my physical body I release into the Mind of God to handle. I accept that my physical body already has perfection within it at the source [God].

This perfection reveals itself through me on every level.

If living richly is your desire, say this: I accept a greater experience of living prosperously. New ways of enjoying life with ease are being revealed through me and my circumstances. I am open to accepting new ideas however big or small. Richer experiences [demonstrations] are coming to me and through me in the form of greater ideas to more fully express my [our] perfect lifestyle. I am open to new people coming into my life. I am receptive to the generosity of others. I experience greater beauty within myself. I am receptive to this abundance flowing into my life from many sources. Nothing is too great or too small for me to accept as a greater experience of richer living.

Step 4: Express GENUINE GRATITUDE for the results that will become real in your future demonstration(s).

After your Step 3 declaration, express gratitude for your expected good, knowing your Treatment is already complete in the greater Mind of God. Believe your demonstration [the expressed goal of your Treatment] is already complete, with the perfect resources to bring it about. Your gratitude is a definite recognition of some good you expect to receive. However, in most instances, your Treatment is subject to the Law of Growth. This universal Law works on your request to bring about the unfoldment of your results here on earth. *This is no time to use your will power, and put away all expectations of others.* Acceptance is your goal. Accept your good is complete in the Mind of God right now. Treatment asserts God is fully aligned with your demonstration and will withhold nothing from you to bring this about. A peaceful change in your mental attitude is a signal your Treatment is complete. In the realm of Spirit [God], your Treatment has already been demonstrated. Begin to feel the peace that surpasses all understanding. After your Treatment is done, push away any doubt. Don't try to take back control or put the brakes on God's activity. It's tempting, but resist. This is your time to go on a mental diet and free yourself of all doubt, worry, and fear.

Step 5: Finally, RELEASE your Treatment, knowing the answer is already complete in the Mind of God. It is of great importance you do this. There is no longer any need to hold back.

When you speak your release, your words resonate with the whole Universe. Your intelligent responsiveness will unify with all Intelligence [God] and work through a Law of Growth to produce your demonstration [results made real]. All resources to accomplish your Treatment are in the Mind of God already. Don't walk away from your Treatment expecting God to now give you something. God instead will give you ideas to act on, one by one. Don't try to negotiate with God, as is often done in traditional prayer.

When you conclude your Treatment say, "And so it is" to show you have released your heart's desire into the Mind of God. Your request has gone from your individual mind to the Universal Mind. Don't pull it back. Don't second-guess, as if someone else can do a better job now. How your demonstration occurs, in what time-frame, what the results might look like, and who should be involved, is up to Universal Intelligence [God] through a Law of Growth. The realization of some good you want for yourself or another may look differently than you expect, but always be in a state of expectancy. Be prepared to experience a shift in your mental attitude or a change in your circumstance. As you conclude your Treatment, proclaim it and name it as yours! **On the following pages, see an all-important summary of the Dos and Don'ts of an effective Treatment. Practicing these will help you immensely improve your results.**

Preparing for a Spiritual Mind Treatment

Your Demonstration Depends on the Words You Use and Thoughts You Think Hourly

When doing a Treatment, keep in mind these Dos and Don'ts. Remember, the Law of Growth is in your life to give you a demonstration. Be laser-focused on bigger ideas and your most important and desired thoughts. DOs and DON'Ts when giving a Treatment ensure you are clearly using spiritual thinking. Re-member the goal is to pray c-o-r-r-e-c-t-l-y. Perfect the language of the Treatment you are doing and in turn you will perfect the results you are receiving.

DOS AND DON'TS OF A SPIRITUAL MIND TREATMENT

DO your Treatment as a daily practice to grow a spiritual con-sciousness. Always remember that God is right where you are, no matter your situation or condition.

DON'T think of God as some far-off deity. Don't separate yourself from this loving presence and feel yourself unworthy.

DO accept the Mind of God is your mind and you are thinking with It right now.

DON'T think answers to your prayers are drawn from only your own limited experience or only from your human mind.

DO think in the clearest terms as you ask for what you want. State unequivocally your desired result. Treatment expresses the qualities of God that you want to experience.

DON'T explain your grievances to God's ear. Don't explain why you believe your good is being withheld or dwell on why it is being delayed. This is a complete and total misuse of your mind. Inferior thinking often starts here.

DO place your request into the Mind of God completely and without reservation. Place your expectations with God, not with a person. The intelligence of God works through a Law of Growth to produce all your demonstrations. All your expectations should be placed into the Mind of God alone. Period. End of story.

DON'T panic and take your prayers back. Don't expect that signs from God can only come in the form of miracles. Relax and know there is a process unfolding in all your demonstrations.

DO let go of lesser conditions. The appearance of an unhappy situation is not a cross to bear. Instead, it is the result of inferior thinking carried over from your past and accepted by you as normal. Lifting your expectations will also lift your spirits.

DON'T dwell on your problems. It is time to fast from all negatives.

DO keep your Treatment between you and God. Privately contemplate what you want. Use this time to enjoy feeling the desired results, even before your demonstration occurs.

DON'T allow naysayers to tell you why your good should be withheld. Don't let them say, "It can't happen to you." It is often best to keep your Treatment private and only with yourself.

DO be thankful and grateful right in the moment you speak your words. Feel confident your good is already complete and in God's care.

DON'T expect results to always be immediate; however, don't discard the fact there are exceptions to this rule, i.e. Jesus the Christ.

DO accept that all your results unfold through an orderly process while you are on this earthly plane. Don't second guess what God is going to do. Know that God's process is orderly and always produces a demonstration. Don't treat your first demonstration as your only one; many demonstrations will reveal themselves when you're looking away. So always look both ways!

DON'T try and pull your Treatment back by thinking you can do a better job. Avoid any use of will power, in any form, to take back control.

Mountaineer Barky says navigating personal growth is always an adventure. Start to see the power of your decisions by staying on a new spiritual footpath. See the power of all your decisions grow as you become more confident in a new way to pray.

Spiritual Mind Treatment puts the answer in every prayer!

**Now, return to page 80 to complete your
Chapter Four Vocabulary.**

Suggested Reading

Barker, Raymond C. *Barkerisms: Potent Statements*, a chronical collected over twelve years by Rev. Dr. Ilomay B. Sims. Published by the author, publishing date unknown.

Barker, Raymond C., *The Power of Decision*. Penguin Books, Tarcher Master Classic Series, 1968, 2011.

Barker, Raymond C. *The Science of Successful Living: Your Spiritual Formula for a Joyous Life*. New York: Dodd, Mead and Company, 1957.

Barker, Raymond C. *Spiritual Healing for Today*. DeVorss & Company, 1988.

Barker, Raymond C., *Treat Yourself to Life: Understanding the Power of Spiritual Mind Healing*. DeVorss Publications, 1954, 1988.

Barker, Raymond C. *You are Invisible: No One Has Seen Your Consciousness*. The Cornwall Press, Inc, 1973.

Emery, Marcia, Ph.D., *The Intuitive Healer: Accessing Your Inner Physician*. St. Martin's Press, 1999.

Federer, Denise, Ph.D., *Working in the Zone*. Federer Performance Management Group, LLC, www.federerperformance.com, 2008.

Fox, Emmet. *The 7 Day Mental Diet*. DeVorss & Company, 1935, 1963.

Holmes, Ernest & Raymond Charles Barker. *365 Days of Richer Living*. Science of Mind Publications, 1953, 2016.

Holmes, Ernest. *Creative Mind and Success*. Church of Religious Science, 1957.

Holmes, Ernest. *Lessons in Spiritual Mind Healing*. Science of Mind Communications, 1943.

Holmes, Ernest. *The Science of Mind*. New York: G.P. Putnam's & Sons, 1938.

Holmes, Ernest. *Your Invisible Power*. Science of Mind Communications, 1974.

Better Ideas for Better Decisions

Subscribe to our free monthly newsletter today!

https://poweryourdecisions.com/#sub

Receive an inspirational article each month to remind you how important fresh new ideas and spiritual practices are to your life. Thoughtful suggestions, new Barky quotes, and a unique Question & Answer column will amplify all the benefits you received from your ***Power Your Decisions*** experience with all the support you need each month to keep making all your best decisions!

All new subscribers also receive a digital collection of six reader's choice articles as a free gift!

FREE NEW TEACHER'S GUIDE TO CREATE YOUR OWN COURSE!

Envision yourself offering a whole generation of decision-makers new and better ways to make great decisions by using this free Teacher's Guide! This guide is simple and easy to follow for anyone interested in creating a study group for *Power Your Decisions Self-Study Workbook*. This opportunity is great for a first-time study group, a book club,or as a refresher course for those who already completed their first self-study! Everyone needs practice, review, and shared experiences to keep the nuggets of wisdom found in this workbook alive! For more information, go to **www.poweryourdecisions.com** to learn how you can order your copy!

Give the Gift of Better Ideas for Better Decisions
Give all your friends, family, and coworkers a free, monthly subscription that will change the trajectory of all their decisions by going to **www.poweryourdecisions.com**.

Bring the Power of Decision to Your Next Event
Dr. Pamela Grey shares her passion for empowering others by offering interactive presentations and workshops to any audience. To book Dr. Grey for your next event, please visit **www.poweryourdecisions.com/speakingengagements**